MW00568426

Table of Contents

The Wizard of 'IS'

The Short, Ugly Story of The Impeachment Of Billy Jeff Clinton and his TrailerPark Presidency

By:

Professor Jerry Mander

ISBN: 0-7392-0272-3

Library of Congress Catalog Card Number: 99-94594

Printed in the USA by

MORRIS PUBLISHING

3212 East Highway 30 • Kearney, NE 68847 • 1-800-650-7888

Legal Notice

This book is NOT intended for consumption by the Humor Impaired or persons not possessing reason. Persons taking this book seriously risk prosecution for Criminal Stupidity. All material contained in this book, with the exception of cited material taken directly from Public Records and News sources, is the creation of the sick mind of the author. All such material represents the opinion of the author. In some cases, created satirical material is enclosed in quotation marks purely to enhance the satirical value of such material and should not be construed to represent actual comments made by the person so satirically 'quoted'.

Furthermore whereas and heretofore therefore the party of the first part wishes it known by all men by these presents ipso facto domino pizzaco. Mea culpa humorus satiricus. Bellagio hotelus penne pasta excellente. Theretowit, carpe diem longus wordium confusium. Endum taurus effluentium.

If you cannot read this you may not sit in an emergency exit row. Please ask the stewardess to reseat you.

About the Author

Professor Jerry Mander is an Unemployed homeless person presently living in Las Vegas, Nevada. Since earning his Doctorate in Political Ethics, Mander has been continuously unemployed. Professor Mander is the originator of the 'dog on a rope' panhandling technique, having completed research that proves conclusively that a 'dog on a rope' increases panhandling revenue by 40% compared with a 'placebo on a rope'. A client of the 'Millenium Homeless Project" which was kicked off in early 1996 by then-respected President Bill Clinton, Mander received U.S. government provided satellite television, a GPS interfaced to an on-shopping-cart portable computer, a cell phone, and voice and email services. These advances in Homelessness have enabled Professor Mander to become Connected and filled with self-esteems. (Previously lacking self-esteem, Mander now has several.)

Diagnosed autistic at the age of three, Mander was found to possess a unique 'savant' gift. Mander knows the Truth when he sees it. His savant gift leaves him unable to interact in "normal' ways. However Mander is able, due to his savant ability,

About the Author. . .

to interpret political speech and 'spin' into everyday truthful speech. The state of autistic homelessness in which he lived prior to his participation in the Millenium Homeless Project left Professor Mander unable to communicate or share his gift.

Becoming connected has allowed Professor Mander, the autistic, homeless, unemployed panhandler, to fully experience the Impeachment of President Billy Jeff Clinton and to write a book about it. Mander, realizing that many working Americans would not have time to follow the events in Washington, decided to write a book that summarized his impressions of the Truth of it. A book that would, in some small way, show his appreciation for all the help he has received over the years in the form of panhandling revenues and government telecommunications equipment and services.

Professor Jerry Mander is a living testament to the success of the Policies of the "Apostle of Progress and Hope", Billie Jeff Clinton.

(You can learn more about Professor Jerry Mander by visiting his Millenium Homeless Person WebPage at www.JerryMander.com)

Forward

The United States of America is the greatest country in the world. We, the people, are the source of that greatness. We, the people, have accomplished wonderful achievements because our Constitution guarantees our freedom and rights. We, the people, have been incredulous that the Impeachment of William Jefferson Clinton has actually been argued with a straight face! I, a people, have decided it is high time to call a spade a spade, a liar a liar, and a fool a fool. I, a people, am gonna have a little fun here. I sincerely hope you, the people, enjoy it.

This book celebrates the participants who provided the hilarity, the fun. Other participants are mentioned only as necessary. For example, the Chief Justice played an important role in the proceedings. But he wasn't necessarily any fun. He would have had to get up during the proceedings and bitch-slap a senator to earn a real place among the group of clowns featured in this book.

Forward. . .

Special thanks go out to Billie Jeff ("B.J.") Clinton, The TrailerPark President, for causing the whole damn thing. And thanks to Hillary Clinton, James Carville, Alan Dershowitz, Larry Flint, Maxine Waters, Barney Frank, Tom Harkin, Hiraldo Rivera and all the rest for enabling a process which has provided the American people and the world with the most hilarious and embarrassing episode in American History. Oh, and thanks to the Press. They avoided asking the tough questions, apparently afraid of losing their places in line at the WhiteHouse Press Buffet Table. The rest of the world is laughing. Laughing at all of them and laughing at us for NOT laughing at all of them. That's about to change.

Let the Dice Fly High! (And may no Sacred Cow remain un-gored)

Let's get you up to speed

To begin to help you understand the TrailerPark Presidency and it's founder, Billy Jeff ("B.J.") Clinton, we will first look over a Timeline of Events and cover a quick overview of our Government and Political System. You will then be introduced to some of the TrailerPark Players. These are the folks who were willing to get right down in the muck to protect Billy Jeff Clinton and the TrailerPark Presidency. The ones who believed they could just spin this all away. There are thousands, but in the interest of brevity, we will profile only the most outrageous and ridiculous ones. We'll look at the most important ones fist, and then, throughout the story, you'll enjoy TrailerPark Player SideTrips to enjoy particularly noteworthy idiocy.

We'll look at the early days of the scandal including a review the Starr Investigation Report. Next we'll move on to the Impeachment of B.J. Clinton by the House of Representatives. We'll look at the Senate Impeachment Trial and examine the Senate Rules and Parts of a Senate Impeachment Trial. We will review the Aftermath of the Impeachment Trial and the Legacy of the TrailerPark President, and then take a quick look ahead into the next Millenium. Finally, you will be provided with Appendix's which outline briefly the Race Card played by Billie Jeff's defenders, and provide a synopsis of the very best of The Presidential Lies.

The story of Billie Jeff 'B.J.' Clinton and his TrailerPark Presidency is a Legacy of Lies and Deceit. A Legacy I'm sure we will all enjoy for years to come. And let's hope that B.J. Clinton enjoys it too. He is, after all, the true author of this, his Legacy.

The Timeline

Here's a listing of key events and dates to help you keep all this organized:

1991: May 8 Governor Billie Jeff Clinton invites Paula Jones to his suite at the Excelsior Hotel and offers her a taste of power.

1993: Nov. 29 Linda Tripp allegedly witnesses Kathleen Willey, 51, emerging from the Oval Office with her makeup smeared and clothing askew. Tripp says Willey told her she had just had an unsolicited sexual encounter with the president.

1994: May 6 Paula Jones Lawsuit filed charging Billie Jeff Clinton with Federal Civil Rights Violations including Sexual Harassment and Defamation of Character.

1995: May Monica Lewinsky graduates from Lewis and Clark College.

June Monica Lewinsky starts work as a WhiteHouse Intern.

November Monica Lewinsky meets Billy Jeff Clinton at a WhiteHouse party. Lewinsky later tells Tripp she has begun having a sexual affair with the President.

December Monica becomes a full-time staff member of the Office of Legislative Affairs.

1997 May 27 The Supreme Court denies the attempt by Billie Jeff Clinton to block Jones lawsuit until after he leaves office.

July Linda Tripp tells Newsweek Magazine about Kathleen Willey leaving the Oval Office in disarray.

August Newsweek magazine publishes Tripp's story about Willey. The Presidents attorney calls Tripp a liar in so many words. Tripp begins recording Lewinsky.

October-November Lewinsky uses Betty Curries contact number for courier services. Six to ten envelopes delivered to the WhiteHouse this way.

November Lewinsky meets with Vernon Jordan at the behest of Currie.

December Tripp is subpoenaed by lawyers in the Jones case. She tells Lewinsky that she will tell the truth. Lewinsky tells Tripp that she intends to lie about the affair. Lewinsky tells Tripp that the President told her not to worry about it because the Jones lawyers would not find out about the affair. She says Clinton told her to deny the affair.

December 26 Lewinsky quits her $32,700 dollar a year job in the Pentagon.

1998: Jan 1 BEGINNING OF THE FIRST INTERMEDIATE PERIOD OF PRESIDENTIAL LIES

Jan 7 Lewinsky files false affidavit in Jones Lawsuit, denying that she was ever alone with the President.

Jan 8 Lewinsky goes to New York for job interviews set up by Vernon Jordan. The interview goes poorly so Lewinsky calls Jordan. Jordan calls Ronald Perelman and then calls Lewinsky back and tells her not to worry. That evening Lewinsky receives a call and is invited back for more interviews. Monica is offered a job. She calls Jordan and informs him and Jordan calls Betty Currie and then the President and announces "mission accomplished".

Jan 10 Willey testifies in Jones lawsuit that Clinton groped and kissed and fondled her in the Oval office in 1993.

Jan 12 Linda Tripp, a Pentagon employee, gives Ken Starr audiotapes of Monica Lewinsky saying she had an affair with the president, which contradicted a deposition Lewinsky gave to Paula Jones' attorneys.

Jan 13 FBI agents wire Linda Tripp for a meeting with Lewinsky. Lewinsky relates a conversation she had with Vernon Jordan in which she says Jordan urged her to lie in her sworn testimony in the Jones case.

Jan 14 Lewinsky gives Tripp a list of 'talking points' for use in Tripp's testimony in the Jones case.

Jan 17 Janet Reno approves Starr's request to expand his investigation to include allegations of perjury and obstruction of justice. Starr's attorneys interview Lewinsky in the Watergate apartment complex. Lawyers for Jones depose Clinton.

Jan. 21 The story breaks: Clinton denies sexual relationship.

Jan 26 Clinton does his famous "I did not have sexual relations with that woman- Monica Lewinsky" routine.

Jan 27 Hillary Clinton reveals "Vast Right Wing Conspiracy."

Feb 15   END OF THE FIRST INTERMEDIATE PERIOD OF PRESIDENTTIAL LIES

Feb 16-July 29-BEGINNING OF THE SECOND INTERMEDIATE PERIOD OF PRESIDENTIAL LIES

July 28 Starr agrees to immunity deal for Lewinsky in exchange for her truthful testimony.

July 30 Lewinsky dress sent to FBI lab.

July 31 BEGINNING OF FIRST INTERMEDIATE PERIOD OF PRESIDENTIAL APOLOGIES
Aug. 6 Lewinsky testifies about White House sex.
August 17 Clinton testifies. On television later admits relationship with Lewinsky that was "inappropriate, in fact, it was wrong".
August 20 Clinton orders military strikes on Sudan and Afghanistan; Lewinsky testifies again before jury. Critics cry 'Wag the Dog'. Sudan and Afghanistan unhappy as well.
Sept. 9 Starr report delivered to Congress; Clinton apologizes again, and again, and again.
Sept. 21 House releases videotape of Presidential testimony in which he looks like a preacher who just got caught with a porn collection. Clinton testifies that he had "inappropriate intimate contact" but denies that the contact constituted "sexual relations".
Oct. 5 Judiciary Committee votes for impeachment hearings.
Nov. 19 House Judiciary Committee opens hearings with testimony of Kenneth Starr.
Dec 15 -END OF FIRST INTERMEDIATE PERIOD OF PRESIDENTIAL APOLOGIES
Dec. 16 Clinton Attacks Iraq; GOP criticizes timing. Iraq not happy either.
Dec. 19 Clinton impeached with two counts, Democrats hold Impeachment Pep Rally in front of the WhiteHouse.
1999: Jan. 7 Senate impeachment trial opens.
Jan. 11 White House denies charges; House files brief.
Jan. 12 Clinton pays Paula Jones off for $850,000.
Jan. 26 The Senate debates in secret.
Feb. 12 Clinton Acquitted by Senate vote.

Understanding our Political System

Understanding the Political System in the United States of America is essential in understanding the Impeachment of B.J. Clinton and the TrailerPark Presidency. Impeachment is not a strictly legal process, you see, it is a political one. So let's look at the structure of our government and the political parties in America.

The Structure of Government in America:

The structure of Government has been likened to a three-legged stool, because our government has three primary parts, the Executive, the Legislative and the Judicial Branches.

The Executive Branch:

The Executive Branch is comprised of, in order of importance, The President (Also known as the Apostle of Progress and Hope), The First Slut, The First Lady, Major Contributors to the President and His Party, The Presidents Friends, and the Vice President. It is important to understand here that the President of the United States is immune from prosecution while actively sitting on the throne, ah...strike that, I meant in the office. Executive Branch officers can only be removed by Impeachment.

The Legislative Branch:

The House of Representatives and the Senate comprise the Legislative branch. The House of Representatives has about 450 members and States get members based upon the census. The Senate is comprised of 100 members, two from each State. The House or Representatives originates legislation in a not so very tactful or collegial process that certainly lacks decorum. The Senate then takes legislation passed by the House and acts upon it very tactfully with collegial decorum. Senators treat Representatives like pond scum while Representatives refer to Senators as 'assholes'. The Legislative Branch is the only branch that can remove a member of the Executive or Judicial Branch. As such, they impeach Judges and Presidents. (Members of the Legislative Branch were considered by the Founding Fathers to be too weak and ineffectual to require removal by impeachment. Especially Representatives, each of which is presently worth less than one fourth of a Senator and one four hundred and fiftieth of a President, at current exchange rates.)

The Judicial Branch:

This Branch is responsible for Re-distribution of Wealth and Power. Advances in modern judicial science have given the Justices the ability to see beyond the inadequate written word of the Constitution, our Laws or the Referendum of the American people. They now have the ability to 'read between the lines' and determine what we really want and need, without even polling us. The Judicial Branch is the definite Branch To Watch in the years ahead.

The Fourth Branch

Traditional texts on the structure of our Government fail to mention the fact that the three-legged stool has grown a fourth leg. The most recent branch of government, the most important Branch to understanding the Impeachment of B.J. Clinton is the **PressnPolls** Branch. The PressnPolls branch of Government is comprised of the Press, many of whom are college graduates, and the Pollsters, most of whom are not. The Press is responsible for asking questions on behalf of the American People, and dutifully reporting the answers, after 'coloring' the news with their own opinions and views. The Polls are responsible for taking Opinion Polls and dutifully reporting the results, after 'coloring' the results with their opinions and views, and getting a second opinion from the Press.

Political Parties

The United States operates as a 'Democratic Republic'. This means that candidates are not elected by a popular vote, as they would be in a true democracy. Instead, our political parties cast *electoral* votes on our behalf. America has traditionally used a *Two Party* system but, in recent years, with the rise of the Libertarians, the Reform party, and Moderate Republicanism, we have evolved our political process into the *Two Party System With StepChildren*.

The Two Parties:

Democrats: The Democrat party is the party of the people. The Democrats are the party that cares about the little guy (as long as that little guy is not too successful). The Democratic Party is the party of Diversity, Civil Rights, Equal Opportunity and Fairness. The Democrat Party is the Party we would all like to let raise our children, if only the forces of Evil would stop Conspiring in a Vast Right Wing Way to prevent it. Democrats supported the President because they understood his weakness, forgave him in a grudging pander to Christianity, and only desire to move forward and get this all behind us and do the work of the American People, but not the Reform Party or Libertarian American People and certainly not the Evil Empire American People. They are the Party of the Apostle of Progress and Hope.

Republicans: The Republican Party is the party of The Evil Empire. Republicans only care about giant multi-national corporations and that silly-ass paper written by old white men called the Constitution. They harp on it continually. They are, in fact, the party of old white men. Mostly old white homophobic white men who are conflicted and suffering from low self esteem. They are the Party of Unfair Attacks upon The Apostle of Progress and Hope. **And, The StepChildren:**

Moderate Republicans: The Moderate Republicans, although members of the Republican Party, are actually 'OK' in a sad, conflicted way. Moderate Republicans are in denial about their own Democratic tendencies. Moderate Republicans may also be referred to as 'Demophobes'. Moderate Republicans support the Apostle of Progress and Hope when they can.

Libertarians: Libertarians are the party for disaffected voters who don't care about winning. Also referred to as the 'Party Who Don't Have any Money, Ha Ha Ha'.

The Reform Party: The Reform Party is the party for disaffected voters who have *some* money and occasionally win. The Reform Party was started by a group of people who were greatly impressed with the use of graphs and other visual aids by Ross Perot. The Party's motto, "Let them eat Pie Charts", has become a clarion call to freedom from spreadsheets.

The TrailerPark Players

William Jefferson Clinton

Born: William Jefferson Blythe, III, Aug. 19, 1946, Hope, Arkansas.

It began in a place called Hope. For Hope, Arkansas was the location of the manger into which young William Jefferson Blythe was born. Like Jesus, William Jefferson Blythe's father wasn't around for his birth either.

William Jefferson Blythe, known as Billy Jeff (or 'B.J.') to his friends, grew up living with his Grandparents, who owned a small grocery store in rural Arkansas. They did business with people of all races despite the segregation so prevalent at the time. "You see", they explained to young Billy Jeff, "no matter a man's race, color or ancestry, you can still take advantage of him, if you lie". Young Billy Jeff never forgot that lesson.

Billy Jeff's mother married a used car salesman named Roger Clinton. Watching his stepfather sell used cars in rural Arkansas as he was growing up greatly affected young Billy Jeff, as did packing up in the middle of the night to quickly move to another town in rural Arkansas. Young Billie Jeff never forgot that lesson. In fact, he changed his last name to Clinton in honor of his stepfather.

The leadership of President John F. Kennedy inspired young Billie Jeff. Young Billie Jeff got the opportunity to meet President Kennedy as part of the 'Boys Nation' program. He was one of the first in line to shake the Presidents hand and was visibly impressed by some of the women he saw around the White House that memorable day. Billie Jeff never forgot that lesson.

That same year, young Billie Jeff was inspired by Martin Luther King, Jr's, "I Have a Dream" speech, which he saw on television. "What a great leader for the black people", he thought, "I wonder if I could even take advantage of him, if I lie?" Young Billie Jeff never forgot that lesson.

And the film, "The Wizard of Oz", inspired young Billie Jeff Clinton. "Did ya see that Wizard guy?" said young Billie Jeff to a friend; "By manipulating people from behind a curtain he was able to control an entire populace of people of different races, creeds and colors, just by lying." And young Billie Jeff never forgot that lesson.

Young Billie Jeff was active in his church and community. Young Billie Jeff was often found to have worked long into the night 'spiritually counseling' with one of the churches young ladies or someone's wife. In fact, young Billie Jeff was so active in his church that, it is reasonable to assume, he was asked to change churches several times. Young Billie Jeff never forgot that lesson.

Billie Jeff was accepted to Georgetown University in Washington, D.C. He chose Georgetown because it had an excellent Foreign Service program; he was also excited about going to school in the nation's capital, remembering being visibly impressed by the women he had seen there so many years before. While earning a Bachelor of Science degree in International Affairs, he worked as an intern in the office of Arkansas Senator J. William Fulbright. There he learned how government worked, where all the private places were in a governmental office, and what it was like to be a politician. And young Billie Jeff, now William Jefferson, never forgot that lesson.

When Bill Clinton finished college in 1968, he desperately needed a way to avoid military service. He won a Rhodes Scholarship, which allows select students to study at Oxford University in England and avoid military service. While at Oxford, he studied government, avoided military service, smoked marijuana, and played rugby. Upon his return to the United States, he began law school at Yale University. At Yale, he continued to work hard. He maintained his interest in government and, it is believed, had several sexual affairs while campaigning for a Senate candidate in Connecticut. He also met Hillary Rodham, whom he would later marry for what certainly appears to have been political reasons.

In 1976, Bill Clinton was elected Attorney General of Arkansas. While Attorney General, Billy Jeff is alleged to have committed a sexual assault on Juanita Broderic at the Camelot Hotel, in what may have been a tribute to John F. Kennedy and his 'Camelot' Presidency. Two years later, at the age of thirty-two, he became the youngest and most sexually active governor in the United States. As governor of Arkansas, he concentrated on improving the state's educational system and building better roads and improving the Highway Patrol Mass Transit System. On February 27, 1980, the Clintons' daughter, Chelsea Victoria, was born. The Clintons describe this day as the happiest one of their lives. Chelsea, almost assuredly, has had occasion to deeply regret it.

By the fall of 1991, Governor Clinton believed that the country needed someone with a new vision and plan, and he decided to run for President. On November 3, 1992, voters turned out in record numbers to cast their ballots. By less than a majority, Bill Clinton was elected the 42nd President of the United States. So Bill and Hillary Clinton packed their grocery sacks, left the TrailerParks of Arkansas behind, and boarded a bus headed off to Washington.

Bill Clinton's inaugural address was prophetic:

"Thomas Jefferson believed that to preserve the very foundations of our nation, we would need dramatic change from time to time. Well, my fellow citizens, this is our time. Let us embrace it. -"

--Bill Clinton Inaugural Address, January 21, 1993

And embrace it he did! Young Billie Jeff Clinton, now restyled William Jefferson Clinton, embraced everything in a skirt, invited or not. For William Jefferson Clinton was now President of the United States, and above the law.

The TrailerPark Presidency had begun.

And to think it all began in Hope.

Hillary Clinton

" *I'm not going to have some reporters pawing through our papers.* **We are the president.**"
Hillary Clinton commenting on the release of subpoenaed documents

Hillary is living proof that America is still great. Look at those pictures of her at the Nixon impeachment hearings. She was a fat, homely little girl. She might have grown up to be some cheesy little slut giving blowjobs to the President of the United States in the White House. But she made good choices and so that fate fell to someone else. She grew up, instead, to become the First Lady of the United States of America.

But that's not the end of the road for Hillary. Hillary Clinton could be the first woman elected to the office of the President of the United States. All she has to do is wait until her husband is out of office and then divorce him and sue his ass for everything he is worth (financially, that is). She would be assured of every female vote in the entire country. What woman could fail to support a woman who 'stood by her man' during his troubles, and then dumped the pig after ripping out his guts in a *really* nasty divorce. It would be a landslide.

This assumes, of course, that the Supreme Court does not rule that Hillary has already served two terms.

Hillary ran into a little trouble in her first term. She had this great health care idea, you see, and got the nod from her co-President to move on it. Got a budget of a hundred grand. Spent about 15 million under that budget and won that years Fiscal Responsibility Award, presented by the Academy of Budgets in Motion. She had a number of 'very successful' secret meetings about the Health Care Plan and then the Vast Conspiracy of the Right Wing cooked up an Evil Witches Brew of dungy allegations that she had violated Federal Open Meeting laws. Oops, turned out they were right. So she let the country see the plan. And the country was not pleased. (Pay no attention to the man behind the curtain.)

Hillary: "Golly, my health care plan has tanked and so has my popularity. I'd better call my hairdresser. A new 'do' will surely distract the press and the public from my Health Care debacle."

Then she was asked to produce some billing documents from the Rose Law Firm, where she had been a partner. Seems the Rose Law Firm had done some work on the Whitewater land scam and they wanted to see if she had worked on it. For two years the documents were lost. Then one day, like magic, they turned up on a table in the WhiteHouse. God knows where those came from! (Pay no attention to the man behind the curtain.)

Hillary: "Hmmm, what are those papers that have been sitting on that table for two years? I think I'll have a look at them. Oh, my gosh, these are those pesky billing records that were subpoenaed two years ago. I'd better give that Special Prosecutor a call right away. I sure hope this hasn't inconvenienced him! Perhaps it's time for a new hairdo."

Then she got in a little tiff for 'allegedly' (snicker, snicker) firing the seven members of the staff of the WhiteHouse travel office and getting the FBI to investigate them. And if that wasn't bad enough, the WhiteHouse counselor assigned to the matter, Vince Foster, up and killed his self. (Pay no attention to the man behind the curtain.)

Hillary: "Oh, gosh, Vince Foster has killed himself. I'd better get my hair restyled."

But Hillary is *really* sharp about money. Hillary dropped a bet and won big in the agricultural futures market. Understand that most people who play in the futures market are VERY sophisticated and specialists in futures. Or idiots, because you can lose your shirt in a heartbeat. But little Hillary Clinton, in her first effort in the futures market, bought an investment and made a hundred thousand on a thousand-dollar investment in just a few days. Just one investment: none before, none after. Wow! Hillary Clinton must have been REAL LUCKY. (Pay no attention to the man behind the curtain).

So Hillary backed off for awhile. Took a sabbatical to find herself. Racked up massive phone bills talking to the Psychic Friends Network. She wrote a book entitled "It Takes a Village." Based upon an African proverb that says that children are the responsibility of the village, not their parents. Kind of a celebration of her roots as the wife of Americas First Black President, who just happens to be White.

Her writing skills now unquestioned, Hillary went on to explore investigative journalism. When it was revealed that her husband, who she knew to be honest, faithful and trustworthy, had been boinking an intern in the oval office, Hillary 'outed' the plot. On January 27, 1998, Hillary revealed that the allegations of sexual misconduct against President Clinton, and the allegations that he coached Monica Lewinsky to lie about it, were the fruits of a *VAST RIGHT WING CONSPIRACY*. Hillary pointed out that the persons involved in setting out the allegations against her husband were right wing, had been stalking him for years, and therefore constituted a right wing conspiracy against her husband. (Pay no attention to the man behind the curtain.)

Hillary went to Sidney Blumenthal and told him that the allegations against the President were completely false. *Sure* Billy Jeff had spent some time with Monica Lewinsky, but the President "ministers" to "troubled people" all the time. It was his "nature". Hillary was clearly, in the opinion of this author, either lying or was the dumbest human being on the face of the planet. (Pay no attention to the man behind the curtain.)

Then came the Blue Dress of Truth. Suddenly Hillary's husband and co-President, little Billy Jeff Clinton, became world-renowned as a lying scumbag, and Hillary was promoted to the status of "victim". Hillary's popularity numbers shot up to an all time high.

Hillary: "Do you like my new 'do' Billy?"
Billy: "It's all disheveled, you look like a rape victim"
Hillary: "No shit, Sherlock."

Hillary took to the role of victim well. No doubt studying old tapes of Princess Di, Hillary adopted the mantle of a wounded woman, and improved upon it. She attended State functions, but always with an expression on her face that clearly shouted, "I'm sitting with a prick! And I can't get up."

And to think it all began in Hope.

Monica Lewinsky

The First Slut. Monica Lewinsky could not have known, at the moment the President of the United States first thrust his johnson at her, that she was simultaneously being thrust into the hot, white light of publicity. But the girl did not seem to mind it at all.

Upon first hearing reports of the Presidents sexual involvement with a "female intern half his age", the American people were not terribly surprised, given his wife, and interested to know more. More about this young, vivacious and, no doubt, sexy temptress who gave herself to his every carnal desire. We had to bet she was hot, having seen Paula Jones and saying to ourselves, "hmmm, except for that nose, not too bad". What sweet young thing was the President dipping into now? Intern. The very word conjured up visions of the most yielding and tender flowers of American youth.

But the Presidential sex life is like a bowl of melted chocolates; he never knows what he's going to stick his finger into next. Door number three opened up and we were shocked. There stood Monica Lewinsky.

Understand that we had figured that the President could have just picked up the phone anytime and 'booty-called' Madonna, or any number of sexy sluts for that matter. We figured that with one phone call and he could have had the 'material girl' and 15 of her closest friends over for more action than even a weary President deserves. The next morning he could have held a press conference on the White House Lawn in his skivvies and announced that Madonna and some other 'friends' were moving in and that Hillary and the American People could just 'kiss his ass' if they didn't like it. That would have been just fine. Clearly not an impeachable offense.

We had assumed the President was stropping some pliant young flower of American beauty and, given his wife, that would have been just fine. Clearly not an impeachable offense.

Hell, the President could have been exploring new sexual horizons with a young *male* intern and that would have been just fine. God knows the American people are not homophobes. And God knows it's not an impeachable offense.

But then we find that the Leader of the Free World is boinking some plain looking Fat Chick. We look at the Plain Fat Chick. We look at Hillary. We look at the Plain Fat Chick. We look at Hillary. We think; "that Hillary must be a worse bitch than we thought."

But there it was: Monica Lewinsky, The First Slut. And now we had to deal with her.

We found out that the President 'liked her smile' and we found out all the wonderful things she did for him as part of their deep relationship. And we began to understand. Blowjobs? Did I understand correctly? Blowjobs? We looked at Monica again, focusing on her smile. And we understood.

Focus on Monica's mouth, and you *know* Monica. For Monica is her mouth. And her mouth is Monica. Monica's mouth has proven to be one of the most powerful forces ever to burst upon the public scene in America. She talked her way into an internship and into the White House and she opened her mouth for Billy and she ran her mouth off about it to just about everyone she knew and then she blabbed a few lies about it under oath and then she got caught and then she blabbed the truth and then she finally shut the hell up awhile after Ken Starr told her she would have to or go to jail. (God Bless Ken Starr for that period of silence we all enjoyed.) Monica Lewinsky is one home-wrecking cow with a world class mouth, any way you look at it.

Ossama Bin Laden looks at Monica Lewinsky's mouth and thanks Allah for unleashing that weapon upon the Great Satan also known as America. Larry Flint looks at Monica's mouth and must wonder if he could, somehow, obtain the services of such a warrior of truth to help him in his quest to search out the Evil Purveyors of the Politics of Personal Destruction. Guys like Alan Dershowitz look at Monica's mouth and wonder why, dear God why; some women tend to forget that wonderful talent on their wedding day.

Many of us became concerned for Monica. How would she bear up under the intense public scrutiny? Would the pressure be too much? Many of us would not have been surprised to awake to headlines that Monica Lewinsky had decided to *blow her brains out*. Her earlier behavior certainly seemed to reveal a propensity for just such a sad end to the slut. But Monica Lewinsky isn't just any slut, she is the First Slut. . . . Our Slut.

James Carville

If a monkey had a mind and smoked about an ounce of crack rock cocaine it would be indistinguishable from James Carville.

James Carville rocketed to public prominence as the Campaign Manager for Billie Jeff Clinton's Presidential Campaigns. Subsequently appointed by the Impeached President to head the Committee Revolting Against the Politics of Personal Destruction (CRAPPD) in 1998, Carville soon had the soul of Joe McCarthy sitting up in his grave and saying, 'cool'.

Ten Things Carville Apparently Wants You to Know

"Civic duty is far from dull these days. In spite of AIDS, there's a lot going on out there when it comes to politics and policy and related sexual activity. You've got to make your voice heard.

The best way, of course, is to vote - and I mean in every election, from the race for dogcatcher all the way up. But voting is not enough. Good Democrats need to roll up their sleeves, unzip their trousers and jump into the mix in many other ways, too.

Here is a simple list of ways you can make a difference:

1. Run for office.

It may seem old-fashioned, but I still believe just about anyone can get elected to office and have a great time. And I'm not just trying to drum up business for consultants; you don't need some overpriced professional liar of a consultant to run your race. Put together your own pack of lies and go for it.

2. Volunteer on a campaign or poll.

If you don't want to run for office, volunteer for someone who does, or get a job as a pollster. There is lots of sex among volunteers and pollsters. Who knows, you may be invited to share a consensual sexual relationship with the candidate! And as a pollster, you not only get a laidback job, you get the feeling of satisfaction that comes from really affecting poll results and public perception.

3. Talk to your children about public affairs and politics.

Make sure your dinner-table talk goes beyond Power Rangers and the prom. Let your kids know that the personal consensual sexual relationships of political persons are just that, *personal.* Teach your children that truth is *relative,* and that honest people can disagree about honesty, *without* being disagreeable. Or wrong for that matter. Civic discussions are too important to be left to people who might be "principled".

4. Write letters to the editor.

Give newspaper readers a chance to read something more interesting than the normal editorial garbage. Write editors posing as a Republican and spout some really radical and unreasonable neo-nazi shit.

5. Go to town hall meetings.

Scandalously few people actually show up at these. Find out where and when you can go. Attend wearing a suit and give that old nazi salute while shouting support for Republicans.

6. Attend school board meetings.

Even if you don't have kids in your local school system, you better believe that what goes on in those schools affects you. Make sure that the textbooks children are exposed to make it clear that truth is *relative*, and that each individual has the right to make up his or her mind about anything without the corrupting influence of "values".

7. Write Members of Congress

In these days of phony-baloney Astroturf lobbying, real letters from real people count. Write letters to your congressman, make 25 copies and sign with different names and addresses (the phonebook can help here). Make your voice heard and make a difference!

8. Write a check.

Sit down with your family or foreign government, decide how much you can afford to give, and get it out there to a candidate or cause you admire. Don't be afraid of Campaign Finance Laws! They may seem clear but those regulations have got words in them like "is" and "alone", if you catch my drift.

9. Get involved in discussions on the Internet.

I'm serious. I hear that that there Internet is a great way to get involved and stay informed.

Here's a **quick list** of ways you can find good Dems in cyberspace:

1. Do a search on the keywords: "LyingPuke' or 'WhiteHouse."
2. Contact the President at Puke@WhiteHouse.gov
3. Visit Democrat Senators at the website of the 'Oath Breakers' organization.

10. Be just as willing to compliment, as you are to criticize.

The last thing we need is the impression of more cynicism. Act outwardly constructive as a democrat. Leave the really rancid crap to me and Larry Flint."

Immediately after the Impeachment of Billie Jeff Clinton, James Carville came out swinging. In a spitting staccato he told the world of the coming Armageddon. He asked America to enjoy the Holidays, go home and kiss the grandchildren, cause come the first of the year there was going to be political blood in the streets-WAHR! The Impeachment of Billie Jeff Clinton went against all that is good and true in America. It went against the POLLS! The American people would RISE UP in defense of their Impeached Liar of a President, BY GOD!

So we all enjoyed our holidays, and kissed our grandchildren. And nobody rose up, nor were there any demonstrations in support of the Impeached Liar President. (Unless you count the Post Impeachment Pep Rally on the WhiteHouse lawn. But that was a gathering of Noses Most Brown and Beholden, and nobody really cared.)

Shortly after the Post Impeachment White House Lawn Pep Rally, James Carville was invited to Israel to run the campaign of Benjamin Netanyahu's challenger. Carville was detained by Israeli customs while attempting to leave the country for allegedly attempting to smuggle antiquities out of the country. After several hours in detention Carville was finally freed and cleared of any wrongdoing when a leading Israeli archeologist confirmed to authorities that skull in question was actually James Carville's own head.

It bears repeating: Give a monkey an ounce of crack cocaine and it would be indistinguishable from James Carville.

David Kendall

David Kendall is the Impeached President's personal attorney and possibly the worst attorney, ever. Just look at what his client has gone through. What a job he has though. A bottomless well of truly interesting legal work. And an occasional leftover babe, I'm sure.

David Kendall always has an odd look on his face. Have you noticed it? A little *strained* look. David Kendall has a closely guarded secret. David Kendall suffers from a little known developmental disorder. He hasn't let it affect his work. He has overcome it, but he must fight it every day.

Look at his face again. Doesn't he have that expression that babies get when they are busy converting a nice clean diaper into a warm, soiled one? If you were properly trained to work in a doctor's world you would know that look for what it is; the symptom of his affliction. You see, David Kendall suffers from 'Arrested Anal Retention Syndrome'.

We all know that Anal Retentiveness is carried on a gene and is an inherited trait. It's common knowledge that Anal Retentiveness (AR) manifests itself as particular talent in such professions as Law, Accountancy and Actuarial Studies. At just a few weeks of age the normal Anal Retentive (AR) gene kicks in, releasing hormones each time the baby poops that direct certain brain cells to form the Anal Retentive (AR) center in the brain. Once the Anal Retentive (AR) center in the brain is fully developed, the recessive gene 'shuts off' the poopal hormone response and becomes inactive. Once this flow of hormone stops the baby does not exhibit the normal "baby *really* concentrating on, and a little bit worried about, taking a successful poop" look on its face while pooping, which is characteristic of normal Anal Retentive (AR) children.

Few know about the gene mutation that occurs but rarely on the Anal Retentiveness (AR) gene. The rare mutation that causes 'Arrested Anal Retention Syndrome', or AARS. For these unfortunate few a mutated Anal Retentiveness (AR) gene never shuts off the hormonal flow. Although enjoying a fully functional Anal Retentiveness (AR) center in the brain, AARS sufferers are constantly bathed in hormones which cause them to continually manifest the expression of a little baby who is *really* concentrating on, and a little bit worried about, taking a successful poop.

Look at David Kendall's face again, and give, to the AARS Institute.

Barney Frank

Rep. Barney Frank is lucky I'm a **homophobaphobe**. Rep. Barney Frank is a proud, gay-flag waving gay man. He stands firm on the rock of the Constitutional Right for a man to blow another man. Or be blown or participate in fanny packing, for that matter. (Note to British readers: that's 'arse packing', in the King's English.) He is Gay and Proud. Proud and Gay. And lucky that I am a **homophobaphobe**.

To understand homophobaphobia you must understand homophobia first. A homophobe is a man who dislikes gays, or disagrees with gays, or finds them distasteful or morally objectionable. A homophobe is really feeling this way because he is, deep within his heart and soul, a raging faggot trapped in a heterosexual body. A homophobe is conflicted. A homophobe only feels the way he does because he *really*, deep inside, wants to drop the soap.

Homophobia may be detected by running the DG (Disagreement with Gays) test. Indications for this test include heterosexual behavior or conservative views. When a patient undergoes this test, the patient's views are sampled by any homosexual who cares to. If the test comes up positive for Disagreement with Gays, treatment is indicated. Treatment involves isolation. The only known cure for homophobia is conversion to homosexuality.

A homophobe is alone. A homophobe has no friends. There is no homophobe support group. There are no government counseling programs available for the homophobe. There is no statute barring employment discrimination based upon homophobia. Shunned by both homosexuals and heterosexuals, the homophobe lives in a nether world of human sexuality. And, once labeled, a homophobe *is* one, unless and until, he takes the cure.

A **homophobaphobe** is a man who is heterosexual and quite comfortable with his heterosexuality. He's looked at the other side and decided, "Hey, the equipment isn't designed to work that way. Guys don't do anything for me. The whole gay thing just doesn't make sense to me." He's heterosexual and he thinks that's Ok. But he lives in fear. His phobia haunts him.

A homophobaphobe is afraid he might be found in disagreement with a homosexual and labeled a homophobe. And in the labeling, be trapped in the limbo world of homophobia, *unless* he takes the cure.

I am such a man.

So Barney Frank gets a pass.

A footnote to Monica:

However, Monica, Barney Frank does provide an example you should pay close attention to. Have you noticed how Barney Frank speaks? His speech is really a mess. I'm sure you've noticed that it's very slurred and difficult to understand. You see some believe that Barney Frank suffers from Repetitive Penile Motion Throat Disorder (RPMTD). Repetitive Penile Motion Throat Disorder (RPMTD) is caused by having a prick jammed down your throat about a half a million times a year. Think about it.

Alan 'Let Me Finish' Dershowitz

Alan Dershowitz is a self appointed defender of the TrailerPark President and his Presidency and the 'Felix Frankfurter Professor of Law' at Harvard University. Funny how some weenies just seem to end up with a label that fits, isn't it? The Felix Frankfurter Professor represents himself as a scholar of the law and the Constitution providing objective analysis on facts and the meaning and action of the law. Instead, some would say, he obfuscates, misrepresents, fabricates or ignores both the facts and the law in some silly-ass quest to explore the boundaries of human gullibility and legal manipulation. Alan Dershowitz apparently hopes to become one of the Great Legal Minds of Our Generation by taking a contrary opinion to any reasonable opinion if it stands a prayer of generating publicity for Alan Dershowitz. Alan Dershowitz might be thought of by some as an ethically bankrupt fool.

While researching on the web I clicked on a link to a site that had Alan Dershowitz as the topic. My browser came back with 'invalid argument'. Talk about your artificial intelligence! My simple little browser program perfectly summed up the totality of Alan Dershowitz: an Invalid Argument.

Alan got the nickname 'Let Me Finish' because of his propensity to grab every bit of airtime possible when given the opportunity to appear on television. He interrupts the opposition continually, then goes on ad infinitum with the most obtuse arguments, occasionally whining, "*Let me finish*" when a more considerate human tries to get a word in edgewise.

Alan Dershowitz authored a book titled 'Chutzpa'. His only obvious purpose in writing the book and naming it 'Chutzpa' was so that he could say, "I wrote the book on it" whenever chutzpa was mentioned. This provides certain insights into his character. Alan's latest book, "Sexual McCarthyism" clearly spells out the case against the Politics of Personal Destruction, an issue of deep and abiding concern to Alan Dershowitz. For Alan Dershowitz is a valiant knight, born to defend the rights of the oppressed.

Let's look at his defense of oppressed O.J. Simpson. Everyone knows that O.J. Simpson left a huge trail from the bloody double murder scene. A six food tall *snail* couldn't have left a better trail. At the sound of ambulances on Bundy Drive Alan Dershowitz and fifty-two thousand other attorneys rushed to O.J. Simpson's side. Sure, O.J. Simpson was entitled to legal representation; no reasonable person would or could deny him that right. But is that really why Alan Dershowitz was there? There were thousands of crooks that could have used Alan's talents. But Alan showed up for O.J. Simpson. To be a Great Legal Mind of Our Generation you have to get in front of the cameras. You have got to get the Good Cases.

Alan's participation in the O.J. Simpson case contributed to the pioneering use of the "Rhyme" defense, now a courtroom classic.

Alan also defended the oppressed Mike Tyson. Mike had found himself embroiled in an accusation that he had raped a woman. In that case Alan unfortunately failed to distinguish himself by introducing the, 'Well, it's not like he bit her fucking ear off" defense. Apparently the timing of the case precluded such a masterstroke. Let's turn to Alan's defense of the President.

Alan seemed to be basing his defense position on the fact that the prosecution:

"Appears to ignore the following important lessons of history:

1. That the overwhelming majority of individuals who make false statements under oath are not prosecuted;

2. That those who are prosecuted generally fall into some special category of culpability or are victims of selective prosecution; and,

3. That the false statements of which President Clinton is accused fall at the most marginal end of the least culpable genre of this continuum of offenses and would never even be considered for prosecution in the routine case involving an ordinary defendant.". . . ."Cops are almost taught how to commit perjury when they are in the Police Academy. Perjury to a policeman - and to a lawyer, by the way - is not a big deal. Whether they are giving out speeding tickets or parking tickets, they're almost always lying. But very few cops lie about the actual facts of a case. They may stretch an incident or whatever to fit it into the framework of the law based on what they consider a silly law of the Supreme Court."

> From Alan Dershowitz' testimony before the House of Representatives.

To summarize; the Felix Frankfurter Professor of Law defends the President by arguing that "Perjury to a policeman - and to a lawyer, by the way - is not a big deal." This defense comes from the author of: **"The Abuse Excuse:Cop-outs, Sob Stories, and Other Evasions of Responsibility"**. So it seems he really **did** write the book on defending the President. Brilliant.

Clearly only an esteemed Felix Frankfurter Professor of Law at Harvard University would be a big enough weenie to have the chutzpa to unload *that* boxcar full of tripe and expect it to fly. Did you notice your pal got IMPEACHED, Alan? (By the way, Alan, I pray that the next cop who pulls you over has heard your testimony and will express his disagreement with you in a very personal way.)

Larry Flint

Larry Flint, confined to a wheelchair every since he was shot by a lunatic who believed he had been told by the loosely translated Voice of God to "Kill that Evil Fuck", is the latest appointee to the Council of Presidential Morality Counselors. Larry Flint is also America's greatest smut peddler. Many Americans might have, at one time, been surprised or even shocked if a President of the United States had associated with a person like Larry Flint. But, understanding that Diversity is the very Cornerstone upon which this Republic was founded; most have come to accept Larry Flint.

For who, among us, is without sin?

Larry Flint has promised to look into that for us. For the American People. Only for the American People, never for himself, and certainly never for the President, who has nothing to do with this. Really. (Pay no attention to the man behind the curtain.)

A one million dollar award was posted by Larry Flint for "Information Leading to Embarrassing Sex Stories on the part of Those Throwing Stones and Posing as Without Sin in Contravention of Larry Flint's Deep Held Religious Convictions". And he hit the mother load. Larry was able to report to the American people that Henry Hyde, Burton Barr and Bob Livingston had all enjoyed extra marital affairs years and years and years ago. And, in the case of Henry Hyde, at least, an affair with quite the tasty dish! Larry Flint was able to demonstrate convincingly that, on a scandal per dollar basis, he would take no back seat to Ken Starr.

Towards the end of the Senate trial it was reported that Larry Flint was hospitalized with some sort of major medical problems of a urological nature. Knowing all we know about Larry Flint's lifestyle, we did not find it surprising that Larry Flint might suffer from major medical problems with his dick.

Senatorial Fatheads

These guys really didn't do anything during the whole impeachment process except do a little camera hogging. And talk about your camera hogging. TV newsrooms go through a mad scramble to find wide angle lenses whenever these guys show up. Combined, these Senators actually have over an acre of head skin between them.

Thankfully, as senators usually act as talking heads on television, we were generally spared any full torso shots on these whaleboys. But can you imagine these two guys in a hurry to get somewhere and colliding? It would make Oklahoma City look like a firecracker.

Of course, we're talking about Senators Ted Kennedy and Senator Jerry Nadler. These two first met over milkshakes and Twinkies at a time when Senator Kennedy was in need of Senator Nadler's special talents. You see Senator Kennedy had this little 'problem' when he spoke out 'About Sex'. Seems representatives of the Evil Empire of the Vast Right Wing Conspiracy would viciously whip up a Witches Brew of Dung each time he did so. Twenty of them would stand up and start singing 'Bridge over Troubled Water' while muttering something about a bridge and a babe. So he needed to stay out of the Limelight. So he needed a mouthpiece. He needed someone who could speak in his place. And for Senator Kennedy to stand behind that voice and not be seen, that voice would have to belong to *one big boy*. Senator Jerry Nadler proved to be just the right guy for the job.

Thus, Senator Nadler was thrust into the spotlight. The spotlight was changed to a flood of dire necessity.

And Senator Nadler began to speak. And he said nothing, absolutely nothing.

Cameraman: "Damn, I'm out of tape and Daschle is ready to spew more irrational tripe again!"
Commentator: "You got that Nadler tape we just made?"
Cameraman: "Yes"
Commentator: "Use that one then, just record over it."
Cameraman: "oh, yea, I must not have been thinkin."

Senator Tom Harkin

Pictures of Senator Tom Harkin may be found in the dictionary if you look up "Empty Suit". Tom Harkin, apparently, does not have the sense God gave a rock.

Tom's contribution to the Senate Trail consisted of posing for Endless Sound Bites and his masterful legal attack on the word "jury". By my recollection it went something like this:

Caring Senator Harkin: *"Mr. Chief Justice, I object!"*

Chief Justice: *"Fine Mr. Harkin, what is it?"*

Caring Senator Harkin: *" I object to being called a 'juror."*

Chief Justice: *". . . .ok . . . .do you care to elaborate on that?"*

Caring Senator Harkin: *"Why yes, as a matter of fact I do. The Vast Right Wing Conspiracy has repeatedly referred to us a jurors and I am prepared to refute that characterization and prove, once and for all, that calling us jurors is not appropriate. I will prove that the word juror does not apply. And I will prove that we are not jurors now, have never been jurors, and are not planning on being jurors in the future and that, finally, 'juror' is a poor word choice."*

Chief Justice: *"jesus"*

Caring Senator Harkin: *"A 'juror', you see, is not what we are. Jurors get box lunches, yet we got no box lunches. Jurors get to get off work, yet we have to come in here every day. Jurors get paid like, five bucks a day for serving yet I see no extra pay for us. Jurors get sequestered which means they get to stay in a motel* *together at government expense and play cards and watch tv, yet there are no motel rooms for us, no tv's. Jurors, , , ,"*

Chief Justice: *"Fine Senator, you've made your point, what would you prefer to be called?"*

Caring Senator Harkin: *"not "jurors".*

Chief Justice: *"Fine, we'll all agree to not call you a juror anymore, anything but juror, that ok with you?"*

Caring Senator Harkin: *"Gee, thanks your honor."*

Chief Justice: *"Senator Harkin, JURORS mistakenly call Chief Justices 'your honor'. Senators call him Mr. Chief Justice, you got that?"*

Caring Senator Harkin: *"Yes, your honor"*

Chief Justice: *"jesus"*

Joe "Curt" Lockhart

Joe Lockhart is the latest in a long string of Presidential Press Secretaries. You see being the Presidential Press Secretary is a very difficult job. They keep having to move on to other jobs when they find out, one after another, what a lying scumbag they work for. I must say, however, that this one looks like a keeper. He doesn't look like he has a single ethical fiber in his body.

Joe "Curt" Lockhart was a charmer right out of the box. One of his first shots at the big time was going in front of the press to cover B.J.'s butt after B.J. started firing off missiles at the Iraqi's in an effort to divert attention from the House Impeachment Proceedings. He started winning friends and influencing people right away with his testy, nay, snotty answers to the press' questions. Even when he wasn't speaking snotty or acting snotty he was *appearing* snotty.

He has a habit of blinking just after a question he doesn't like is asked of him. It's not just a quick little blink. It's kind of a slow, purposeful blink. It's a slow, purposeful, dismissive blink. It really seems to be communicating in a non-verbal way with anyone who asks a difficult question, and that communication is not a nice one.

Detailed analysis of video footage of Joe "Curt" Lockhart using sophisticated National Security Agency type equipment finally identified the reason his blinks were so bothersome to so many people. Joe "Curt" Lockhart has the words 'Fuck' and 'You!' micro-tattooed on his right and left eyelids, respectively. The micro-tattoos are too small to be read normally. However, his blink cycle permits the subliminal transmission of his message.

Take a good look at him at his next news conference. Watch for the blinks and ask yourself, "What was the message he just sent to me and the rest of the American people?" Now that you have been sensitized to his subliminal messaging it will be clear to you. A simple message to America from the President; "Fuck You".

ABOUT SEX

Throughout the investigation, impeachment and the Senate trial of B.J. Clinton we continually heard, "This is all About Sex!" from the Democrats and "This is not About Sex, It's about Perjury" from the Republicans. You decide, and we'll talk more about this later. But for now, we have to dive into it. You see, it certainly all started with sex. It started years ago with young Bill Clinton banging any skirt that looked his way. While going to school, while dodging the draft, while kissing all the right butt and putting on airs to further his political aspirations. Getting lots more when he got to be a Governor and could get the highway patrol to leave the driving to them. Kept doing it after it started to get a little messy. Couple of allegations popped up that were a bit embarrassing. Women he'd done kept popping up and whining and he had to do a few favors to shut them up. And he kept doing it. There was a Federal Civil Rights Lawsuit filed about it against the President, and he kept doing it.

You can only conclude that Billy Jeff Clinton has a **serious** hankering for some pussy. And that's why it all started About Sex.

Put on your rubber gloves and gird your loins. To find out if it really was "About Sex" you must, as part of your civic duty, immerse yourself in the 'good bits'. First, a quick look at Billy Jeff's smooth and sophisticated way with women that got him into the Paula Jones Civil Rights Lawsuit; then we'll look at the Starr Report.

Paula Jones Deposition (edited to remove the boring bits while preserving the romance)

BY MR. BENNETT:
Q. Mrs. Jones, on May 8th, 1991, you went to a room in the Excelsior Hotel where you met Governor Clinton; is that correct?
A. That's correct.
Q. And how long were you in the room total?
A. Between 10 and probably 15 minutes.
Q. And did you voluntarily go up to the room?
A. With the guidance of a state trooper, yes.
Q. And why did you go up to the room?
A. Because I wanted to meet the governor and he wanted – he asked to meet me.
Q. And why did you want to meet the governor?
A. Because it was exciting. I had never met the governor before. It's exciting. So I was going to go up there.
Q. And I believe you've stated publicly that you thought maybe it would help you get a better job; is that right?
A. That's correct.
Q. How long were you in the room before you first saw the governor's exposed penis?
A. Probably about five – between five and six or seven minutes.
Q. Do you remember ever seeing his penis without his hands on it?

A. Yeah. I saw it. Because when he pulled his pants down, I saw it without his hands on it and I saw what it looked like.

Q. And then his – one or two hands were on it?

A. Yeah. Because he pulled his pants down with both hands and when he sat back, I mean, it's there and then he starts putting his hands all over it.

Q. All right. And what was he doing?

A. He was fondling himself.

Q. Did he have an erection?

A. Yes, he did.

Q. What did you do as soon as you saw that?

A. I jumped up and I said, "I'm not that kind of girl," after I looked at it and he was trying to grab me. But, I mean, I went on ahead and jumped up and I turned around and that's when I – that's the thing I drew there from this perspective of standing up, looking down on the couch at him.

Q. So you didn't see it before you stood up?

A. Yes. I looked at it. It was pointing my direction. But when I stood up, it was pointed to the left.

Q. So then –

A. So.

Q. You stayed in the room for another five or 10 minutes?

A. Oh, no. I started to leave. And he pulled up and I was fixing to go out and I said, "I've got to be going. I've got to go back to the registration desk. I'm going to get in trouble." He pulled up, you know, stood up. And he was just red as he could be. You could tell I had embarrassed him so bad, because he probably expected me to do something. And he pulled up his pants, trying to situate himself. And I don't think he tucked in his

pants. He just pulled them up and zipped his
pants up, still with an erect penis.
And he said, "Well, you know, if you have any
trouble, I want you to have Dave Herrington
call me immediately." And that was the second
time he had mentioned Dave Herrington. And
then I proceeded to go on to the door and he
rushed up behind me. I started to open up the
door, he put his hand on the door to where I
could not open it up any further, and he
stopped me and he says, "You're a smart girl,
let's keep this between ourselves." And when
I went out the door, the state trooper was
there, which is Trooper Ferguson. And he was
standing out there.
Q. Are you saying that the governor did not
let you go out the door?
A. Not for a split second, yeah. He confined
me for a moment to let me know
that I'm a smart girl and let's just keep
this between ourselves.
                    From Paula Jones Deposition

   Please note the description by Paula Jones of the
presidential member. It seems that his member is a pretty
good representation of Billy Jeff as a person. They both
could be described as "a prick that leans to the left".

   After reading Paula Jones testimony we should be
starting to get a sense of this guy's character and style.
All you guys that have been wondering how you could be
more successful with the ladies; pay close attention. Billie
Jeff Clinton has got this romance thing down; and you
would be well served to be taking a few notes.

Just remember Billie Jeff's mnemonic, **RDPIL**. Get them in a *R*oom, drop *D*rawers, fondle *P*enis, *I*ntimidate them if you can and *L*ie if you need to. **RDPIL**. It may not work every time, but it's quick and efficient.

The Starr Report (edited to for brevity but preserving the good bits)

The following information is reported as a Public Service to the millions of Working Americans who were unable to find the time to wade through the Starr Report to find the good bits.

Friendship (Nov 15, 1995)
"What began as a friendship"
        According to B.J. Clinton

"According to Ms. Lewinsky, she and the President kissed. She unbuttoned her jacket; either she unhooked her bra or he lifted her bra up; and he touched her breasts with his hands and mouth. Ms. Lewinsky testified: "I believe he took a phone call . . . and so we moved from the hallway into the back office . . . . [H]e put his hand down my pants and stimulated me manually in the genital area." **While the President continued talking on the phone (Ms. Lewinsky understood that the caller was a Member of Congress or a Senator), she performed oral sex on him.** *He finished his call, and, a moment later, told Ms. Lewinsky to stop. In her recollection: "I told him that I wanted . . . to complete that. And he said . . . that he needed to wait until he trusted me more. And then I think he made a joke . . . that he hadn't had that in a long time."*
        From the Starr Report(emphasis added)

Some friendship, huh! Remember that this is the first time these two stoats have ever been alone together. We particularly enjoyed the part about Billie Jeff talking to a member of congress while Monica worked her magic. White House phone records revealed he talked to Rep. Jim Chapman while he introduced Monica to the Digital Revolution and to Rep. John Tanner while Monica resuscitated the Presidential Pestle.

Getting to Second Base (Nov. 17, 1995)

(B.J. asks Monica to bring him some pizza. She delivered the pizza and he gave her a tip.)

"Ms. Lewinsky testified that she and the President had a sexual encounter during this visit. They kissed, and the President touched Ms. Lewinsky's bare breasts with his hands and mouth. At some point, Ms. Currie approached the door leading to the hallway, which was ajar, and said that the President had a telephone call. Ms. Lewinsky recalled that the caller was a Member of Congress with a nickname. While the President was on the telephone, according to Ms. Lewinsky, "he unzipped his pants and exposed himself," and she performed oral sex. Again, he stopped her before he ejaculated.
During this visit, according to Ms. Lewinsky, **the President told her that he liked her smile** *and her energy."*
From the Starr Report (emphasis added)

Boy, I *guess* he liked her smile! So far he seems to think her smile is waaaay ok.

White House phone records revealed he talked to Rep. H.L. "Sonny" Callahan while being serviced. (Suspected phone conversation content: "*Hey Sonny, betcha can't guess what I'm doing right now.*")

Happy New Year! (Dec. 31, 1995)

"*According to Ms. Lewinsky, they moved to the study. "And then . . . we were kissing and he lifted my sweater and exposed my breasts and was fondling them with his hands and with his mouth." She performed oral sex. **Once again, he stopped her before he ejaculated because, Ms. Lewinsky testified, "he didn't know me well enough or he didn't trust me yet.**"*

From the Starr Report (emphasis added)

Didn't *trust* her? Did I hear that right? He didn't *trust* her? He puts his member in her mouth and he doesn't *trust* her? He's got his finger on the button of the largest nuclear arsenal in the world and he puts his willie in the mouth of someone he doesn't trust? What in the hell does he do with people he *trusts*??? (Belay that, I'm sure it's best we never know).

Thinking about taking up a Nasty Habit (January 7, 1996)

"*Ms. Lewinsky testified that during this bathroom encounter, she and the President kissed, and he touched her bare breasts with his hands and his mouth. The President "was talking about performing oral sex on me," according to Ms. Lewinsky. But she stopped him because she was menstruating and he did not. Ms. Lewinsky did perform oral sex on him. Afterward, she and the President moved to the Oval Office and talked. According to Ms. Lewinsky: "[H]e was chewing on a cigar. And then he had the cigar in his hand and he was kind of looking at the cigar in . . . sort of a naughty way. And so . . . I looked at the cigar and I looked at him and I said, we can do that, too, some time."*

    From the Starr Report (emphasis added)

Getting queasy here. Monica menstruating is simply more than any of us wanted to know.

Monica Gets a Ring and a Date....(January 21, 1996)

"We had . . . had phone sex for the first time the week prior, and I was feeling a little bit insecure about whether he had liked it or didn't like it . . . . I didn't know if this was sort of developing into some kind of a longer-term relationship than what I thought it initially might have been, that maybe he had some regular girlfriend who was furloughed . . . .
According to Ms. Lewinsky, she questioned the President about his interest in her. "I asked him why he doesn't ask me any questions about myself, and . . . is this just about sex . . . . or do you have some interest in trying to get to know me as a person?" The President laughed and said, according to Ms. Lewinsky, that "he cherishes the time that he had with me." She considered it "a little bit odd" for him to speak of cherishing their time together "when I felt like he didn't really even know me yet." They continued talking as

they went to the hallway by the study. Then, with Ms. Lewinsky in mid-sentence, "he just started kissing me." He lifted her top and touched her breasts with his hands and mouth. According to Ms. Lewinsky, the President "unzipped his pants and sort of exposed himself," and she performed oral sex.

At one point during the encounter, someone entered the Oval Office. In Ms. Lewinsky's recollection, "[The President] zipped up real quickly and went out and came back in . . . . I just remember laughing because he had walked out there and he was visibly aroused, and I just thought it was funny."

From the Starr Report (emphasis added)

Can you *believe* these two pigs? This is in the White House of the United States of America and his wife and daughter live there.

Venus and Mars...(Feb 4, 1996)

"There, according to Ms. Lewinsky, they kissed. She was wearing a long dress that buttoned from the neck to the ankles. "And he unbuttoned my dress and he unhooked my bra, and sort of took the dress off my shoulders and . . . moved the bra . . . .

[H]e was looking at me and touching me and telling me how beautiful I was." He touched her breasts with his hands and his mouth, and touched her genitals, first through underwear and then directly. She performed oral sex on him.

After their sexual encounter, the President and Ms. Lewinsky sat and talked in the Oval Office for about 45 minutes. Ms. Lewinsky thought the President might be responding to

her suggestion during their previous meeting about "trying to get to know me." It was during that conversation on February 4, according to Ms. Lewinsky, that their friendship started to blossom.
     From the Starr Report (emphasis added)

There is a definite Venus and Mars thing happening here. You see; B.J. Clinton is a Mars and he thought their friendship bloomed the first time he got her alone and got her to give him oral sex. (Come to think of it, not too many men would argue that position.) But Monica, you see, is a Venus. She had to keep giving him oral sex for months until she felt he was getting to know her before she could feel that their friendship was starting to blossom. Clear proof that the whole Venus and Mars thing applies even to the famous and powerful. Or those giving head to the famous and powerful, for that matter.

Breaking Up is Hard to Do...(Presidents Day, Feb 19, 1996)

"In Ms. Lewinsky's recollection, the President telephoned her at her Watergate apartment that day. From the tone of his voice, she could tell something was wrong. She asked to come see him, but he said he did not know how long he would be there. Ms. Lewinsky went to the White House, then walked to the Oval Office sometime between noon and 2 p.m. (the only time she ever went to the Oval Office uninvited). Ms. Lewinsky recalled that she was admitted by a tall, slender, Hispanic plainclothes agent on duty near the door.

The President told her that he no longer felt right about their intimate relationship, and he had to put a stop to it. Ms. Lewinsky was welcome to continue coming to visit him, but only as a friend. He hugged her but would not kiss her."
From the Starr Report

He hugged her but he would not kiss her. This was a hopeful time. B.J. Clinton has found the strength to exercise will power over his natural instincts. After only two and a half months of a gutter relationship B.J. "no longer felt right" about being serviced by a slut in the house he shared with his wife and daughter. Indeed, he was proving himself to be a man of honor and a pillar of good taste. Hey, he slipped up; any man could with such an exotic temptress as Monica Lewinsky. But here he is, stepping up to the plate. Being *strong* for the wife and kid, and for America, *never* for himself, *always* giving. God, don't ya just love that man?

A Matter of Taste (March 31, 1996)
*"In the hallway by the study, the President and Ms. Lewinsky kissed. On this occasion, according to Ms. Lewinsky, "he focused on me pretty exclusively," kissing her bare breasts and fondling her genitals. At one point, **the President inserted a cigar into Ms. Lewinsky's vagina, then put the cigar in his mouth and said: "It tastes good."** After they were finished, Ms. Lewinsky left the Oval Office and walked through the Rose Garden."*
From the Starr Report (emphasis added)

This is the man who wants us to be upset about Joe Camel? One can only suspect by his behavior that the President is beginning to trust Ms. Lewinsky, at least around the humidor. And, what the heck, the Surgeon General never said you could get AIDS from a cigar. Right, Mr. President?

Happy Easter Mr. President! (April 7, 1996)

"He told me that he thought that my being transferred had something to do with him and that he was upset. **He said, "Why do they have to take you away from me? I trust you."** *And then he told me -- he looked at me and he said, "I promise you if I win in November I'll bring you back like that." ….*
When asked if he had promised to get Ms. Lewinsky another White House job, the President told the grand jury:
What I told Ms. Lewinsky was that . . . I would do what I could to see, if she had a good record at the Pentagon, and she assured me she was doing a good job and working hard, that I would do my best to see that the fact that she had been sent away from the Legislative Affairs section did not keep her from getting a job in the White House, and that is, in fact, what I tried to do. . .
. **But I did not tell her I would order someone to hire her, and I never did, and I wouldn't do that. It wouldn't be right.**
After this Easter Sunday conversation, the President and Ms. Lewinsky had a sexual encounter in the hallway, according to Ms. Lewinsky. She testified that the President touched her breasts with his mouth and hands. According to Ms. Lewinsky: "I think he

unzipped [his pants] . . . because it was sort of this running joke that I could never unbutton his pants, that I just had trouble with it." Ms. Lewinsky performed oral sex. The President did not ejaculate in her presence.
During this encounter, someone called out from the Oval Office that the President had a phone call. He went back to the Oval Office for a moment, then took the call in the study. The President indicated that Ms. Lewinsky should perform oral sex while he talked on the phone, and she obliged. The telephone conversation was about politics, and Ms. Lewinsky thought the caller might be **Dick Morris.** *White House records confirm that the President had one telephone call during Ms. Lewinsky's visit: from "Mr. Richard Morris," to whom he talked from 5:11 to 5:20 p.m."*

From the Starr Report (emphasis added)

Remember that Billie Jeff Clinton, (Southern Baptist?!?), had gone to church that Easter morning with his loving spouse. He waltzed out of church, waved to the cameras, got in his limousine and rode back to the WhiteHouse with his little woman. Then he got together with the First Slut and they played the home version of the resurrection. All while he was on the phone with Dick Morris. Funny when you think about it. Both the President and Monica were, in a manner of speaking, orally interacting with a dick. Actually, the person the President was talking with was orally interacting with a dick as well. You take a call from the President and you could be involved in a threesome for all you know.

But although he now trusts her, he still can't find release. It must be his constant worry and concern for the American people. The weight of office hangs heavy over the President. Concerned *only* with the work of the Presidency, the Apostle of Progress and Hope cannot let go. Monica has to be wondering, " *Is it me, or him?*"

In his Grand Jury testimony B.J. says, "*But I did not tell her I would order someone to hire her, and I never did, and I wouldn't do that. It wouldn't be right.*" Just when did this keenly developed sense of right and wrong develop?

Wake Up Calls July 19, 1996

"According to Ms. Lewinsky, the President telephoned her at about 6:30 a.m. on July 19, the day **he was leaving for the 1996 Olympics in Atlanta, and they had phone sex, after which the President exclaimed, "[G]ood morning!" and then said: "What a way to start a day."** *A call log shows that the President called the White House operator at 12:11 a.m. on July 19 and asked for a wake-up call at 7 a.m., then at 6:40 a.m., the President called and said he was already up.* **In Ms. Lewinsky's recollection, she and the President also had phone sex on May 21, July 5 or 6, October 22, and December 2, 1996. On those dates, Mrs. Clinton was in Denver (May 21), Prague and Budapest (July 5-6), Las Vegas (October 22), and en route to Bolivia (December 2)."**

From the Starr Report (emphasis added)

Phones and Sex, Sex and Phones. There is a definite Phones and Sex thing going on here. The President seems to be using the phone and having sex and having sex while on the phone and having phone sex; a lot. I personally wouldn't be surprised to see Clinton propose an Alexander Graham Bell Memorial right next to the Lincoln Memorial.

The President: "Hi, I'd like to get a room please."
Motel Clerk: "Yes Sir, will it just be you two in the room."
The President: "Yep, just me and my wife here, Mrs. Smith"
Motel Clerk: "that'll be $19.99'
The President, winking at 'Mrs. Smith': "Does the room have a *phone*?"

Happy Valentines Day! February 14, 1997

"On February 14, 1997, the Washington Post *published a Valentine's Day "Love Note" that Ms. Lewinsky had placed. The ad said:*
HANDSOME
With love's light wings did
I o'er perch these walls
For stony limits cannot hold love out,
And what love can do that dares love attempt.
-- Romeo and Juliet 2:2
Happy Valentine's Day.
M

From the Starr Report

Did the silly slut really think this relationship was *love?* Blowjobs in the workplace and phone sex and the fat dolt is quoting *Romeo and Juliet?* This is a dolt whose greatest intellectual goal is probably trying to find out how many fat grams are in the average load of semen and she thinks this trashy servicing agreement is romance.

   Monica Lewinsky does not even qualify as a bimbo. Bimbo's are typically cute and loveable but stupid. Monica Lewinsky not particularly cute and is so apparently stupid that her stupidity must be an embarrassment to all the stupid people who have ever lived.

Monica Gets a Wad of Bills (Feb. 28, 1997)

"Ms. Lewinsky described the Whitman book as "the most sentimental gift he had given me . . . it's beautiful and it meant a lot to me." During this visit, according to Ms. Lewinsky, the President said he had seen her Valentine's Day message in the Washington Post, and he talked about his fondness for "Romeo and Juliet."

Ms. Lewinsky testified that after the President gave her the gifts, they had a sexual encounter: [W]e went back over by the bathroom in the hallway, and we kissed. We were kissing and he unbuttoned my dress and fondled my breasts with my bra on, and then took them out of my bra and was kissing them and touching them with his hands and with his mouth. And then I think I was touching him in his genital area through his pants, and I think I unbuttoned his shirt and was kissing his chest. And then . . . I wanted to perform oral sex on him . . . and so I did. And then . . . I think he heard something, or he heard someone in the office. So, we moved into the

bathroom.
And I continued to perform oral sex and then
he pushed me away, kind of as he always did
before he came, and then I stood up and I
said . . . I care about you so much; . . . I
don't understand why you won't let me . . .
make you come; it's important to me; I mean,
it just doesn't feel complete, it doesn't
seem right.
Ms. Lewinsky testified that she and the
President hugged, and "he said he didn't want
to get addicted to me, and he didn't want me
to get addicted to him." They looked at each
other for a moment. Then, saying that "I
don't want to disappoint you," the President
consented. **For the first time, she performed**
oral sex through completion.
When Ms. Lewinsky next **took the navy blue Gap**
dress from her closet to wear it, she noticed
stains near one hip and on the chest. *FBI*
Laboratory tests revealed that the stains are
the President's semen."
          From the Starr Report (emphasis added)

From the description of that dress it seems like the
President must have gone off like the Puffed Rice Cannon!
I particularly like the part about the moral dilemma faced
by Monica. No, you sick soul, not that one! The moral
dilemma she faced when she articulated, " *I care about you
so much; . . . I don't understand why you won't let me . . .
make you come; it's important to me; I mean, it just
doesn't feel complete, it doesn't seem right*". (Reader tip:
Say her quote to yourself in the voice of Scarlet in 'Gone
With The Wind'. What theatre, the human mind.)

Monica may have been saved further degradation had
she just paused to think. (We learned that from one of

those B.J. Clinton sponsored Anti-Drug Commercials they've been broadcasting at us). Would that Monica had thought to seek help at that moment. She might have thought to herself, '*I mean, it just doesn't feel complete, it doesn't seem right, gee, I am faced with moral dilemma. To whom should I turn? Hmmm, isn't there a radio talk show host who helps people like me solve moral dilemmas?*" (Reader tip: Keep her in the Scarlet voice in your head, it really adds to the scene.) Instead of Monica being further degraded it may have, had she turned at that crossroads of life, gone something like this:

Radio Talk Show Host: "I'm Dr. Laura Slashinger and my number is 1-800
D R, B I T C H, that's 1-800 D R, B I T C H; Let's take our first call, Hi . . Monica! You're on the air"
Monica: "Hi Dr Laura, I just first wanted to tell you how much I admire your show"
Dr. Laura: "Well Thank You! And what can I help you with today?"
Monica: "Well Dr. Laura, for several months now I have been giving oral sex to a married man in his home office where I work for him and he won't let me make him come, I mean, it just doesn't feel complete, it doesn't seem right."
Dr. Laura: "So you're saying you're a peter-puffing, home-wrecking slut and it doesn't seem right to you, You find that *surprising*".
Monica: "Well, yea, I guess so.....but I just thought it would be all right if he would let me make him come"

Dr. Laura: "So what do you want me to tell you? That you need to try some of that peppermint flavored oil on him and maybe shove an ice-cube up his butt? You think I'm going to tell you how to make him come using oral sex? I'm a married Jewish woman for Christ's sake! I haven't done that since I got married. The simple fact is that you are acting like a slut and it will never feel right until you buy one of my books."

Monica: "How much are they?"

Dr. Laura: "$29.95 and that includes shipping and handling"

Monica: Well, I can't afford that right now. I'm just an unpaid intern in the WhiteHouse."

Dr. Laura: "Perhaps there is someone in your life who would give you one of my books as a gift in spite of the fact that you are obviously a low-life home-wrecking slut."

Monica: "Well, yes, maybe I could ask the President to give me one."

Dr. Laura: "Yea right Monica, and while you're at it maybe you could write a book about your skanky ways and make a few million bucks. You need therapy. You are sick and delusional in addition to being an immoral tramp. You need to get some help."

Monica: "Hmmmm...I like your idea about a book. Thanks, Dr. Laura."

Dr. Laura: "I'll tell you what, Monica. You stay on the line and I'm going to give you one of my books for free. You really need it."

Monica: "Thanks Dr. Laura, but I think I'll just go with your book idea instead."(click)

Dr. Laura: "Thank you, Monica, for your call. Wow, was that girl a mess or what? Just shows how screwed up you can get if you act like a whore.
I'm Dr. Laura Slashinger and my number is
1-800 D R, B I T C H.

The Plot Thickens

"According to Ms. Lewinsky, she had what proved to be her final sexual encounter with the President on Saturday, March 29, 1997. Records show that she was at the White House from 2:03 to 3:16 p.m., admitted by Ms. Currie. The President was in the Oval Office during this period (he left shortly after Ms. Lewinsky did, at 3:24 p.m.), and he did not have any phone calls during her White House visit.
According to Ms. Lewinsky, Ms. Currie arranged the meeting after the President said by telephone that he had something important to tell her. At the White House, Ms. Currie took her to the study to await the President. He came in on crutches, the result of a knee injury in Florida two weeks earlier.
According to Ms. Lewinsky, their sexual encounter began with a sudden kiss: "[T]his was another one of those occasions when I was babbling on about something, and he just kissed me, kind of to shut me up, I think." The President unbuttoned her blouse and touched her breasts without removing her bra. "[H]e went to go put his hand down my pants, and then I unzipped them because it was easier. And I didn't have any panties on. And so he manually stimulated me." According to Ms. Lewinsky, "I wanted him to touch my

genitals with his genitals," and he did so, lightly and without penetration. Then Ms. Lewinsky performed oral sex on him, again until he ejaculated.

According to Ms. Lewinsky, she and the President had a lengthy conversation that day. He told her that he suspected that a foreign embassy (he did not specify which one) was tapping his telephones, and he proposed cover stories. If ever questioned, she should say that the two of them were just friends.

If anyone ever asked about their phone sex, she should say that they knew their calls were being monitored all along, and the phone sex was just a put-on."

From the Starr Report (emphasis added)

Does this guy lie or what? A foreign embassy tapping the phones? Golly, that could really interfere with a Presidential sex life! Let's do this next one to Pink Panther music.

The Oval Bedroom

Hillary: *"Billy, we need to talk."*

Billy: *"Sure hon, what's on your mind"*

Hillary: *"You never seem to want to make me have sex with you anymore. And it's happened before. What's wrong, Billy? You're not screwing around again, are you?"*

Billy: *"Well, ah, I hadn't wanted to worry you dear, but, well, it's like this. I believe a foreign government, or maybe some drug guys, are broadcasting radio waves at me to take away my sexual drive."*

Hillary: *"Oh, my god!"*

Billy: *"They've been doing it for years, off and on. But I didn't want to worry you. You know how I am about protecting you and our little Chelsea."*
Hillary: *"You **are** a fine man, Billy Jefferson Clinton."*
Billy: *"Oh, thank you hon."*
Hillary: *"G'night Billy"*
Billy: *"G'night Hilly"*
Hilly: *"Billy?"*
Billy: *"Yes, hon?"*
Hilly: *"I just want you to know I don't mind about the radio waves taking away your sex drive. I know that in spite of it you love me as much as you ever have."*
Billy: *"You're right about that Hilly."*
Hilly: *"G'night Billy"*
Billy: *"G'night Hilly"*

May 24: Break-up

"On Saturday, May 24, 1997, according to Ms. Lewinsky, the President ended their intimate relationship. Ms. Lewinsky was at the White House that day from 12:21 to 1:54 p.m. The President was in the Oval Office during most of this period, from 11:59 a.m. to 1:47 p.m. He did not have any telephone calls. According to Ms. Lewinsky, she got a call from Ms. Currie at about 11 a.m. that day, inviting her to come to the White House at about 1 p.m. Ms. Lewinsky arrived wearing a straw hat with the hat pin the President had given her, and bringing gifts for him, including a puzzle and a Banana Republic shirt. She gave him the gifts in the dining room, and they moved to the area of the study.

According to Ms. Lewinsky, the President
explained that they had to end their intimate
relationship. **Earlier in his marriage, he
told her, he had had hundreds
of affairs; but since turning 40, he had made
a concerted effort to be faithful."**
From the Starr Report (emphasis added)

Hundreds of affairs! We *were* impressed. B.J.
Clinton is quite the swordsman. One hopes that the rest
of the legion of Presidential pleasers were better looking
than the one B.J. soooweee'd up from the pen for this
affair.

So there you have it, in all its salacious detail.

The Starr Investigation: Forty Million Bucks (OH MY!!)

Ken Starr was appointed Special Prosecutor in 1994. For four years the poor man did the dirty nasty stinking smelly shit work of investigating the President and the TrailerPark Presidency. Poor Bastard. Poor Innocent Bastard.

Can you imagine what he went through? His job was to search out the truth of any Criminal wrongdoing in the WhiteHouse. Think of the Truth as a herring. Think of lies as red herrings. Think of Ken Starr's job as a search for a herring, in a sea of red herrings. You keep setting your nets and pulling them in. And you get nothing but red herrings. NOBODY tells the truth. Getting sent off to find 'The Criminal' in the WhiteHouse is like getting sent off to find 'The Problem Gambler' in Las Vegas. Everyone looks like it and acts like it; but nobody will *admit* it. Hillary, it does not take a Vast Right Wing Conspiracy, it takes one person telling the truth and a blue dress with your co-liar's semen on it.

Too much has been made of the FOURTY MILLION dollars (Oh MY!!) spent by the Starr Investigation. But read the depositions and watch the videos on the Impeachment and Trial. Sifting through that typhoon of lies on only 40 million is actually quite the bargain. Works out to about sixty cents a lie by my reckoning.

But still: Forty Million bucks sounds like a lot of money to the average American. And it is. But let's put it in perspective. There are really two angles to consider.

First, was there any result from the Starr investigation? Second, lets look at some other waste incurred by the TrailerPark Presidency.

RESULTS OF THE STARR INVESTIGATION:
The Impeachment of B.J. Clinton:

If anyone doubts the American people supported *this* Result of the Starr Investigation then let's put a little check box on the new tax forms. "Check here if you want one dollar of your taxes to go towards the Impeachment of B.J. Clinton." I'll bet dollars to donuts that 40 million Americans would check the box.

WhiteWater:

In this Result of the Starr Investigation former Arkansas governor Jim Guy Tucker was convicted in 1996 of Fraud and Conspiracy. He got four years to think about it but his sentence was suspended because his doctor testified that he would die of liver disease if imprisoned. On Feb. 20, 1998, Tucker pleaded guilty to avoiding $3 million in income taxes due on a sham bankruptcy in the 1980s and agreed to cooperate with Whitewater prosecutors who wanted information about the Clintons.

James and Susan McDougal were also a Result of the Starr Investigation. Susan McDougal was sentenced to two years in prison. She went to prison on contempt charges because she declined to testify against the Clintons even though she was granted immunity. Seems Susan had signed a check for almost six grand that noted "Payoff Clinton" in the 'remarks' line. She declined to tell what Clinton was being paid off for. James McDougal was sentenced to three years in prison for conviction on 18 fraud and conspiracy charges, but died of a heart attack before Bubba the jailhouse bully could have his way with him.

Webster Hubbell's resignation from the Justice Department and subsequent conviction was another Result of the Starr Investigation. In March 1994, Webster Hubbell, a former law partner of Hillary Clinton's, resigned from the Justice Department as associate attorney general before pleading guilty to fraud and tax evasion while in private practice. After the plea bargain, Clinton's buddies funneled an estimated $700,000 in 'consulting' work to Hubbell. Starr's office opened an inquiry into whether White House aides or associates of the Clinton's, including Vernon Jordan Jr., arranged payments to Hubbell to ensure his silence on Whitewater matters. (Pay no attention to the man behind the curtain.)

Hubbell was convicted of fraud and served 18 months in jail. On April 30, 1998, Hubbell, his wife and their attorney and accountant were charged with tax evasion.

But that's not all! When you listen to the B.J. Clinton SpinMaster 2000 avoiding the facts you get more! Seems that Ken Starr and his team have thus far won 9 guilty pleas, 3 jury convictions, seen 2 defendants partly acquitted with a mistrial on other counts and has several indictments and trials pending.

So it seems the Starr investigation *did* have some Results beyond the Impeachment of B.J. Clinton. The entirely non-partisan defenders of B.J. Clinton must have inadvertently forgot to mention that while bitching up a storm about the Forty Million Dollars (Oh My!).

Clearly the whole forty million must not have been spent only investigating the President. However, we will go ahead and pretend to believe it was for awhile, in order to avoid being sidetracked into ridiculous arguments with the defenders of the President, who are not prepared to defend the President using anything resembling facts or logic.

But let's put that forty million dollars in perspective. It was, after all, government expenditure. To put forty million government dollars in perspective, think of it as equivalent to the cost of a single sheet of toilet tissue in your household budget. And the President and his TrailerPark Players used lots of toilet paper. Lets look at some examples.

WASTE IN THE TRAILERPARK PRESIDENCY

President Clinton spent **300 bazillion** of our tax dollars on his anti-drug advertising campaign. You know, the old 'Your Brain on Drugs', 'Reefer Madness', type of thing.

I remember sitting at home one night thinking, " *I've never tried it before, but perhaps I should run out and score some crack or heroin and get high, high, high tonight after I get the kids to sleep*". One of those commercials came on and the impulse just died. I know *I'm* a believer in the effectiveness of those ads now. Perhaps, given the power of advertising, we could ask the Impeached President to spend an extra couple of hundred thousand for commercials that would address his little problems. They could be run on the televisions at the White House (or the Big House, for that matter) just for him.

Image of boxing Speedbag, just hanging there.
Announcer: "This is your willie, Willie"
Video Image of Mike Tyson working out on the Speedbag, furiously
Announcer: "And this is your willie getting slapped around by the press, you fat, stupid puke"
Fade to Black Screen with Text: "Keep your willie to yourself, Willie"
Brought to you by the Partnership for a Puke Free WhiteHouse.

Or maybe one to help him get his legacy in proper perspective;

Image of Office Tower
Announcer: "This is your Legacy"
Image of Office Tower being imploded
Announcer: "And this is what you did to your legacy, you complete, economy-sized, TrailerTrash moron."
Fade to Black Screen with Text: "How could you be such an incredible ass."
Brought to you by the Partnership for a Puke Free WhiteHouse.

More Waste

Hillary Clinton spent **15 million** of our tax dollars on her dismal failure of a 'Health Care' plan. Seems the budget of $100,000 just wouldn't cover a few necessary extras. (By the way, just when did *she* get elected? Did I miss something?)

Hillary Trips: The phrase "women's issues" is defined in the First Lady Handbook and Training Course as equivalent to "shopping". Air Force One is listed in the Inventory section as "Shopping Vehicle-Government, 1 ea." Remember when Hillary and little Chelsea went to India to bask in women's issues? Do you remember their little jaunt to Africa for the same purpose? Can you imagine how much that cost? A 747 for a week or so. Secret Service personnel, entourage, fighter escorts for Airforce one. Do you know that it costs about $50,000 an *hour* to run a modern jet fighter? That's one fighter jet for one hour. And they sip gas compared to Airforce One. You *know* that those trips cost us ten or twenty million each.

But, to be fair, we all must admit to the benefits that we saw flow like manna from heaven from those trips. I know my awareness that women were meeting in India and later in Africa to discuss women's issues increased at least, oh, several hundred bucks worth.

Any way you cut it the forty million spent by Starr was a bargain. Compare it to the amount of our money B.J. and the Family and friends hosed away or look at the results. Ken Starr should get the 1998 Government Fiscal Responsibility Award.

Impeachment

On September 9, 1998 Kenneth Starr presented his Report of the Independent Counsel to the House of Representatives. Ken Starr's report included 11 charges against Billie Jeff Clinton, including perjury and obstruction of justice. The Starr Report also included some of the most interesting testimony, in a sick sort of way, seen this side of an old skanky favorite 'Hustler' magazine.

We got phonesex and oral sex and the oval office and we got cigars and we got the President of the United States of America just lying about it and lying about it. We got the President of these United States getting back gifts and making up stories and getting that girl a *good* job. We got a President that has been lying to EVERYONE about all of this for months now. We got a President that we KNOW would never have admitted any of this if a blue dress with his semen on it had not suddenly appeared. It's apparent that the President of the United States, the Chief Law Enforcement Officer of the United States, started lying about all this to defeat a Federal Civil Rights Lawsuit against him, and then kept on lying about it, up to and including lying under Oath before a Grand Jury.

Based upon the facts presented, the House of Representatives could have, in good faith, impeached his ass the next morning. But just to be sure they were fair, they opened Hearings into the matter.

The House Judiciary Committee assembled. Prosecution Managers were appointed. Ken Starr's massive report was read and reread and highlighted and had its corners folded late into the night. As the House prepared for the Hearings mineral water was ordered and the toilets in the House restrooms were 'Sanitized for Your Protection.'

The Prosecution presented their case. Damn! It really appeared to be overwhelming evidence that the President of the United States had committed Perjury and Obstruction of Justice. There were about 60,000 pages of evidence, to be exact. There may have been a couple of minor points for the attorneys to quibble about, but any reasonable person who read the files would be forced to conclude that the President had sure run roughshod over the law.

But, of course, we had not yet heard the Defense. The Presidents counselor, David Kendall, repeatedly and vociferously made it clear that he would be bringing forth witnesses that would clear the good name of Billie Jeff Clinton. As the world waited in anticipation mineral water supplies were flown in and the House restroom toilets were again 'Sanitized for Your Protection.' (If you are familiar with some of the more 'Light on His Feet' Representatives you understand how essential this is to the efficient operation of the House of Representatives. Rest assured that nobody takes a crap in the House without first inspecting to insure that those seals are intact. It's a Health Care thing. It's not a Homophobia thing, it's just good Health Care.)

The Presidential Defenders list included, among others, the following luminaries; their defense arguments are summarized for brevity:

PANEL I: Historical Precedents and Constitutional Standards

Gregory B. Craig, Esquire, Assistant to the President and Special Counsel

Acted as the Master of Ceremonies.

Honorable Nicholas Katzenbach, (Former Attorney General of the United States)

In a telling argument, pointed out that the Presidents Poll numbers were good. The Ultimate Defense against Impeachment.

Bruce Ackerman, Sterling Professor of Law and Political Science, Yale University

Convincingly argued that the Impeachment would have to be thrown out because the 105th House of Representatives had adjourned and the 106th had been convened. Clarified that Federal Judges could, should and had been impeached for Perjury but that the President was "different". Argued that "High Crimes and Misdemeanors" could not include little 'ol felonies like Perjury and Obstruction of Justice without, of course, getting into the "Misdemeanors" part too much.

Sean Wilentz, The Dayton Stockton Professor of History, Princeton University

Described the Representatives who would vote to impeach the President, or have anything to do with it, as "Profiles in Cowardice". Pointed out that the President had "dishonored his Presidency", but that he had apologized for it. Warned the members of Congress that they would "darken" their reputations if they supported impeachment. Spoke about his '500 historians agree' petition in which 500 historians agreed that Clinton's crimes were not impeachable, leaving out the part about the 500 historians being mostly, not historians.

Samuel H. Beer, Eaton Professor of the Science of Government Emeritus, Harvard University

Advised that the Congress should consider the President's "whole record" and not focus in on the actions for which he was being impeached. Implicitly concluded that the Presidents 'whole record', which should be considered, should not include any records like the Starr Report or the Jones Federal Civil Rights Lawsuit or getting blown in the Oval Office while on the phone to a Congressman, or any of the litany of Presidential Lies.

PANEL II: Abuse of Power

Honorable Elizabeth Holtzman, Former Member of Congress from New York

Articulated that she, as a Former Member of Congress, didn't think the President had abused his power. Seemed to have worked hard to convince herself about it.

Honorable Robert J. Drinan, S.J., Former Member of Congress from Massachusetts

Presented the "Apocalypse Defense". Convincingly argued that the Impeachment of Billie Jeff Clinton would "paralyze" and "immobilize" the nation. Persons exposed to this defense became convinced that, given that fact that Drinan is a cleric, there might be Prophecy foretelling this in the book of Revelation. Father Drinan judiciously avoided any references to "Priests" or "Altar boys" during his arguments.

Honorable Wayne Owens, Former Member of Congress from Utah

Really nailed down the issue of "Personal and Private" acts of a President as opposed to "Official Acts" of a President. I mean, it's not like the President issued an Executive Order requiring Monica Lewinsky to blow him, was it? And it wasn't like the President, as Commander in Chief, ordered himself as a member of the Armed Services to perjure himself or Obstruct Justice, was it? 'Nuf said.

PANEL III: How To Evaluate Evidence

James Hamilton, Esquire, Swidler, Berlin, Shereff & Friedman, Washington, DC

Pointed out that "High Crimes and Misdemeanors", according to Alexander Hamilton, "relate chiefly to injuries done to society itself". Thankfully spared us his logic in concluding that the past **Year of National Bullshit** we have endured had nothing to do with the actions of the President and has not, again thankfully, been injurious to society.

Richard Ben-Veniste, Esquire, Former Assistant U.S. Attorney

Led the "If You Can't Attack the Evidence, Attack the Prosecutor" Defense. Presented clear and convincing evidence that Ken Starr had "tortured" Billie Jeff Clinton and pointed out that Ken Starr was "aggressive" and lacked "proportionality". He did this in the same argument in which he spoke forcefully against partisanship, hypocrisy and sensationalism. To understand his argument you needed to use both your 'left brain' and your 'right brain', and then link them together in your 'hind brain'.

So there it was, complete refutation of the charges against the President. **Case Closed**.

Oh, there were other witnesses, and a few hundred spin miesters and blah, blah, blah boys and girls. It started with the 'They got No Case' crew, then came the 'It don't Rise to the Level of Impeachable Offenses' crew, followed by the 'Censure and Move On' crew.

The Censure crew was really the most fun. The proposal amounted to putting a note in the President's Permanent File that the President would agree to. It couldn't, of course, say anything really concrete, or the President wouldn't agree to it. The Censure would look something like this:

Hear Ye! Hear Ye! Know all Men by These Presents! The Congress of the United States of America Hereby <u>*Rebukes*</u> William Jefferson Clinton, <u>*Stingingly!*</u>

Imagine THAT in your permanent file! Whooweee. Sends chills right up your spine.

So the House of Representatives got together and called for the vote. And when the guilty votes were counted they included the votes of several Democrats who had crossed party lines in a clear show of Partisan Politics. An 'lil Billie Jeff Clinton became the first President in the History of the United States of America to be IMPEACHED.

And to think it all began in Hope.

The Senate Trial

With the vote to impeach the president in the House of Representatives the baton of justice was passed to the Senate. And the Senate took that baton, knowing that history would be watching and that, on a matter of tectonic political weight, only *they* could act.

And act they did. Senators were pushing and shoving to get in front of the television cameras so they could reassure America that they were a collegial group filled with decorum and tact. There would be none of the partisan contentiousness and rancor that had marred the House of Representatives.

Then they went into the Senate Chamber, and without contention or rancor, they began the work of the Senate. They researched the Constitutional issues and the precedents and crafted Rules for the trial. And they agreed by a vote of 100 to nothing on those Rules. The bipartisanshipness of it was simply stunning.

Let's go into the Senate Chamber and listen in on the Secret Senate Deliberations that resulted in this incredible show of bipartisanship and collegiate tactful decorum (Senators will be described rather than named to preserve the secrecy of the meeting):

Senator of the Evil Empire: "We'll call the meeting together. Sergeant at Arms, have the doors been sealed and has the room been cleared?"

Sergeant at Arms: "Yes, the room is secure, Sir."

Senator of the Evil Empire: "Ok, listen up, we have got to come out of this chamber with an agreement or the press is going to chew our ass.

Bottom line is this, there are 55 of us and 45 of you and there is, by God, gonna be a trial. Clinton is guilty. We all know it. The evidence against him is just a clear as videotape and his defenses are some of the lamest ass legaling we have ever seen. We all know that so lets not waste any time in here discussing it. That being a given, about 45 of you don't give a damn about the facts or the law or your oath and would pimp your nieces to bail Billie Jeff Clinton out of this mess. So this is what we're going to do. Right now we are going to agree to convene a trial and listen to the House prosecution managers and the President's defense arguments. We'll give em three days each. We'll decide about witnesses once we've seen how the poll numbers react to that. How's that sound?"

Caring Senator: "Hey Trent, that sounds great. I really like the idea of getting a feel for how the polls look before we really get into this. I support the idea."

Senator of the Evil Empire: "All those in favor."

100 Senators: "Aye"

Senator of the Evil Empire: "ok, the meeting is adjourned then."

Caring Senator: "Hey Trent"

Senator of the Evil Empire: "Yes, Tom"

Caring Senator: "We really need to get this over quick. Wouldn't you agree?"

Senator of the Evil Empire: "You bet. Do you realize that for as long as this trial goes on we have to actually come in to work on time every day and sit in our seats without talking and we can't even fall asleep because all the cameras will be going?"

Caring Senator: "That's no lie, this is going to be hell."

Senator of the Evil Empire: "No Kidding."

Senate Trial Rules

The Senate Trial, according to the rules passed by the
Senate in that incredible show of collegially tactful
decourous bipartisanshipness, consists of two distinct
parts. The First Part of a Senate Trial in Six Parts, also
referred to as the **Bipartisan Appearances Phase**, and the
Second Part of the Senate Trial, also known as the
Partisan Phase. The **Bipartisan Appearances Phase** of a
Senate Trial is comprised of, in order of importance, The
Polls, The State of the Union Address, The Papal Visit,
The Prosecution, The Defense, and Another Secret
Meeting. The **Partisan Phase** of the Senate Trial consists
of Three Pitiful Witnesses, Closing Arguments and The
Final Secret Meeting.

Bipartisan Appearances Phase of a Senate Trial, Part I- Polls

Much has been made of the poll results, which continued to show 'widespread approval' and 'support' for B.J. Clinton throughout the investigation and impeachment and senate trial. You say, " **Hey**, they never polled *me!*" Not surprising. You see these polls are typically taken using a thousand or so samples, which are then statistically extrapolated to the population at large. Can't you see it? You ask a thousand people a question and you learn what 270 million are thinking. Upon hearing that the average citizen might say something like, "hey, that sounds like a load of crap". The intelligentsia would immediately, and with no small sense of urgency, set upon such citizen. Pummeled by the pervasive arguments of several college educated pundits with laptop computers, the un-polled 269,999,000 (no pun intended) of us slink back into our corners, forever appreciative that someone has been able to tell us what we think.

My college statistics professor introduced the topic of Statistics with the following:

> "*Statistics is like a bikini, it reveals the titillating while concealing the essential*"
>
> (My college statistics professor, whose name I have forgotten, although he was a really cool, nutty professor looking sort of a guy. By now I'm sure he has been removed from office for saying such a horrid sexist thing on a college campus, poor guy. I do hope he's doing well.)

Let's consider a few *flaws* in the polls.

Polls poll everyone

Everyone doesn't vote. In fact, only about 40% of the citizens of the U. S. are registered voters and in the last election only 37% of those registered voters actually voted!

Assume for a moment that those citizens who do vote are more active politically than the non-voters. That should not be too great a leap. Further assume that EVERY VOTER in the country wanted the TrailerPark President impeached and removed from office for being such an incredible lying puke. Now take your poll. Call a thousand citizens at random and ask your question. Now write your headline/soundbite:

'SIXTY PERCENT OF AMERICANS SUPPORT B.J. CLINTON AND DO NOT WANT HIM IMPEACHED'

Did you see how that worked? The sixty percent you reported supporting B.J. are the non-voters. You factually reported the titillating while the essential remains hidden. Cool, huh?

People are not colored balls

Pollsters assume people are colored balls. If you have one opinion you are, let's say......blue! If your of another opinion we'll say you are.....green! (I personally like picking the colors and find it exciting, as you may discern.) Pollsters poll and you only get to be one color or another. However, and sadly for the pollsters, people are not colored balls. On a given matter some are blue, some are green, some are blue/green with and emphasis on the green, some are blue/green with an emphasis on blue and some are red and some are completely colorless and some people just don't care. Let's listen in on one of those telephone polls, shall we?

RIIIINNNNGGG
RIIIINNNNGGG
RIIIINNNNGGG
Citizen: 'hullo?'
Pollster: 'Hello and good evening. I'm calling on behalf of the Organization for the Making of Money by Conducting Polls by Interrupting Your Dinner and Selling The Results and I was wondering if you would mind taking a few minutes to answer our important poll questions.'
Citizen: 'FUUUUUCCCCCKKKK **YOU**!', <click>
Pollster: 'green ball'

The hard truth of the matter is that if you don't care you don't count. But always remember that the completely untrained and unprofessional pollster who calls you can count you any way he sees fit anyway.

The Clue Impaired

Pollsters assume that all men are equal. I could have said 'people' out of deference to the feminists, but they can kiss my butt after the way that they continued to support B.J. Clinton in spite of his repeated sex-harassing infringement of peoples civil rights, particularly in the case of his lying in the Paula Jones *federal civil rights* lawsuit. The feminists, and particularly that ugly hog Betty the 'Oink' 'Oink' Friedan, proved that they are intellectually and ethically bankrupt and the whole world knows it. Wake up and hear the laughter Betty, you putrid troll. But I digress.

Pollsters assume all men are created equal. Only those who have never caught an episode of 'The Jerry Springer Show' can hold an assumption like that to be valid. Speaking of which, we can well imagine an episode featuring Hillary and Monica bashing the dickens out of each other with chairs while B.J. Clinton sits back with a cocky smile and says to the audience, " *I can't help it, they both want what I got, hehe*". Again, I digress.

The Clueless simply don't count. The Constitution provides for our equality and all True Americans agree with that. De Jure (in law) we are all equal and should all count in polls. De Facto (in fact) the Clueless don't count and should not be included in polls. Let's listen in on another call:

RI I I INNNNGGG
Clueless Citizen: 'hullo?'
Pollster: 'Hello and good evening. I'm calling on behalf of the Organization for the Making of Money by Conducting Polls by Interrupting Your Dinner and Selling The Results and I was wondering if you would mind taking a few minutes to answer our important poll questions.'
Clueless Citizen: "Sure"
Pollster: "Do you support the Impeached President or do you want him removed from office?"
Clueless Citizen: "what office?"
Pollster: "The Presidency"
Clueless Citizen: "huh?"
Pollster: <click>, "green ball

The hard truth of the matter is that if you don't have a clue you don't count.

The Bias Factor

The Art and Business of the Making of Money by Conducting Polls by Interrupting Your Dinner and Selling The Results can allow the results to be skewed by the way a question is phrased.

Contrast the following minor variations in wording and imagine the effect on poll results:

Pollster 1: "Do you think the President should be removed from office for misleading a couple of people about an embarrassing affair to protect his wife and his dear sweet innocent young daughter?"

Pollster 2: "Do you think the Impeached President should be removed from office for repeatedly lying to the public, a Grand Jury and to the Congress and Obstructing Justice: or would you prefer to see him sitting in the oval office for the next couple of years getting blowjobs from interns while talking on the phone to your Congressman?"

See? It's *how* you ask the question.

The Confidence Factor

When they tell us poll results the pollsters tell the press and the press tells us and there is a little something lost in the translation. The press tells something like, "63% of Americans don't want the Impeached President convicted and removed from office and that is accurate within plus or minus 3%". That sounds pretty damn convincing, doesn't it?

What the statisticians *really* told the press was, "63%, for results based on the total sample of adults nationwide, one can say with 95% confidence that the margin of sampling error is no greater than +/- 3 percentage points." That '95% confidence' number is the kicker.

The 95% confidence factor is the one generally used in statistical reporting. Apparently the press is either incapable of understanding it, thinks it's too complex for our simple and innocent minds, or assumes we all know about it and understand it. It would be great if we could assume that they assume we all know about it and understand it. But I'm afraid that the confidence factor on our assuming that would be one weak number.

I'm telling you: that confidence factor, it's the kicker.

Lurking in that innocent missing little 5% is the chance that the poll is WAY off. And that's assuming the poll was performed without error or bias using clearly phrased questions. Take that little 5% apart and lurking way over there in the right hand corner is a nasty little 1%. Do you see it? Way over there on the right. That little 1% tucked away in the corner. I'm telling you that little 1% lurking over there is one mean little widow-making bastard. That little guy can rock your statistical world. That little 1% contains the *certainty* that the Poll is worth about as much as a Presidential Promise, and is about as trustworthy as a Democrat Senator's oath to do impartial justice.

Meditate on this, Grasshopper.

We Never Seem to Learn

Even the best pollsters blow it. But we keep listening to them like a bunch of sheep. Jesse Ventura was NEVER gonna be Governor of Minnesota according to them. But it sure seems they miscounted their colored balls on that one. (Congrats and best wishes, Jesse, btw. And congrats to the non-sheep who ignored the polls and voted for you).

Remember that famous picture of Harry S. Truman holding up the headline announcing "Dewey Wins"? That's was the 'sure loser' President Harry S. Truman holding up a Chicago Tribune headline that was obviously written by someone who trusted the polls.

The Last Word on Polls and Polling

I searched the Internet on January 18, 1999 using Lycos and the words "Gallup Poll". What follows is a direct copy of result el numero uno. I kid you not.

```
Gallup Poll
The Gallup Poll NOW HIRING! Data Collection
Specialist Great part-time or full-time job
for students or homemakers. Great second job.
Relaxe.
http://www.creativeloafing.com/mall/gallup/in
dex.h
Similar Pages | More pages from
creativeloafing.com
```

Get the picture?

The Last Numbers on Polls and Polling

Let's have little fun. Let's introduce the factors noted above into the pollsters' results. Pretend we just did a poll about something and the result came out to 70% plus or minus 3% 'For' something related to politics. **Everybody doesn't Vote** is clearly worth a plus or minus of 55%. For **People are not colored balls,** we'll give a couple of percent. **The Clue Impaired** should be worth at least plus or minus 5%. We'll give the **Bias Factor** plus or minus 5% and nobody is going to tell me there is no bias. If we add the original plus or minus three percent to our quite reasonable adjustments we get plus or minus 70%.

Betty Danewslady: "The latest poll results are in that show support for the Impeached President to be at an all time high of 70%"

Peter Danewsguy: "Betty, what's the plus or minus on that?"

Betty Danewslady: "It's plus or minus 70%, Peter, That's 70%, plus or minus 70%"

Peter Danewsguy: "Of course that's at a 95% confidence factor and assumes that little 1% lurking over in the corner of the missing 5% isn't out partying after making some statistician cry. Right, Betty?"

Betty Danewslady: "That's right, Peter. And now in related health news, hundreds were sickened at an East Coast nude beach where Harvard Law Professor Alan Dershowitz was reported vacationing."

The Scary Part

The Scary Part is that nobody seemed to notice that poll results went real-time during the trial of B.J. Clinton. One thousand U.S. citizens chosen at random were wired into a poll network connected to computer terminals in the WhiteHouse and press-rooms across the country. Twenty-seven minutes later Wall Street introduced Presidential Futures and Congressional Options.

The Bipartisan Phase of a Senate Trial Part II: The State of the Union

On Tuesday, 19 Jan 1999, President Clinton gave his State of the Union address. In the midst of the Senate trial, which would determine his fate and the fate of the Nation, the Impeached President courageously strode out in front of both houses of Congress and the American people to do the work of the President.

That State of the Union address turned the tide of Impeachment. The following day the Impeached President's public opinion polls notched even higher, rivaling Amazon.com for the most highly valued unfulfilled promise in the history of the known universe.

The State of the Union Address was a Masterpiece.

Verbal Content Analysis

Masterfully crafted, the State of the Union Address cleverly avoided the use of easily misunderstood words like 'is' and 'alone'. Subjected to computer word count analysis, the Address revealed that the third most common word used was 'children.' (After "sorry" and "oops", his earlier 2,468 apology speeches having been incorporated by reference.). The fourth most commonly used word was 'freebie'.

Before we move on, let's take a moment to consider some prophetic words:

"The government consists of a gang of men exactly like you and me. They have, taking one with another, no special talent for the business of government; they have only a talent for getting and holding office. Their principal device to that end is to search out groups who pant and pine for something they can't get and to promise to give it to them. Nine times out of ten that promise is worth nothing. The tenth time is made good by looting A to satisfy B. In other words, government is a broker in pillage, and every election is sort of an advance auction sale of stolen goods." [H. L. Mencken]

Think on this, Grasshopper, as you consider the following:

The Bait of the Union Address

You're a President in deep shit. You've been Impeached and the Senate trial is in progress. The facts are sure not on your side. But you have some good public opinion polls. Who you gonna call? When the going gets tough, the political toughs get giving. The Bait for the Union Address offered something for everyone. In it, the Impeached President spent like Imelda Marcos on the day she found out the 13th pair was free.

You see, the Impeached President held a trump card. Our Money. That's right, Our Money. Our Money in the form of a huge budget surplus generated by his sponsoring the massive tax increases we bought into like fools a few years ago. Huge piles of Money. Huge piles of Our Money. Trillions of dollars of Our Money. And in The Bait for the Union Address he used most of it to bribe virtually every voter group in the country. He didn't really give it back. That would be a tax reduction or a refund. He didn't suggest that the surplus be used to pay down the national debt. (Excuse me, but wasn't that one of the reasons we let them pass that massive tax increase in the first place?) No, if you're a President in deep shit, you use that money to buy votes.

(Thought exercise: Imagine you are a scam artist and you have stolen an aging couple's entire life savings. Should you, A: give the money back to the old folks and ask that they forgive you and hope they might ask the judge to be lenient upon your conviction after you plead guilty or, B: Tell the old people that the money is *gone*, they will never see a *dime* of it if you are convicted, but if they were to, say, *seek to influence the jury*, you would give them a *gift* of having their gas turned back on and paying the bill for the winter, and perhaps a nice warm meal once in awhile? If you answered 'A' go directly to jail. If you answered 'B' you are qualified to run for office.)

It's essential that you be clear in your understanding of our Surplus. Let's take a break here for some homework on that pesky topic. After you have read 'Understanding Our Surplus', we'll get back into the details of the Bait of the Union Address.

Understanding Our Surplus

The key to Understanding Our Surplus rests on the Essential Cornerstones of Government Finance. Government Finance is just like personal finance, it's just got a lot bigger numbers. Once your understand the Sources and Uses of Government money, it's just as easy as managing your personal budget at home.

Sources of Government Money

Taxpayers: Under our system of Government, the taxpayer is the citizen with which the Government has a deal. The deal is, roughly, "You give me (insert percentage here) of your money every year or I will take away everything you own, including putting your children in a foster home, and put you in jail."

Government Borrowings: This is the National Debt we hear so much about. Government Borrowings occur when the Government goes to taxpayers or foreign governments and says, "Here's the deal, lend me money to spend. I promise to pay you back with money I get from taxing my citizen/taxpayers later. I wouldn't be bothering you but I can't get away with taxing them anymore right now." Currently the National Debt is a number that only Carl Sagan understands, although skeptics have voiced skepticism that he actually does.

Uses of Government Money

Government Expenditures: Under our system of Government, a government expenditure is a spending of the money taken, or to be taken, from citizens/taxpayers.

As you can see, the basics are pretty simple. But there are few *complications* like:

Social Security: Social Security is another deal between the Government and the Taxpayer. This one, simplified, says: "You give me an additional (insert percentage here) of all the money you earn or pay in payroll or I will take away everything you own, including putting your children in a foster home, and put you in jail. But; I will give you money when you retire for this one."

The Government takes this Social Security money and spends it. First, to make payments to the first Social Security recipients, then on whatever it wants. (Reader tip: Do a web search on the keyword "Ponzi" for a further explanation of this financing technique.)

The Social Security Fund, you see, has no actual money in it. It represents the Government's Promise to Pay. In essence, the Government takes our money to spend, promising to remember to pay us, but doesn't save any money. When it needs to pay us to fulfill it's promise to pay us, it turns to its' Source of Funds, the taxpayer. *To summarize: the Government tax upon us for Social Security is in exchange for its promise to pay us with money it will raise by taxing us again, later.* (So let's all get behind the President and Save Social Security)

Occasionally the Government finds that it has inadvertently taxed us more than even the Government ever dreamed it could spend. It has taxed us even more than even the Government thought we would stand for without rising up to overthrow the government. This is a **Surplus**. And a Surplus is a *crisis* in government, requiring immediate attention to see that it does not remain unspent.

To put all this in human terms, imagine the Government as a very big older brother. Your older brother takes half of your allowance every week, threatening to beat your ass if you don't pay. At the same time, he is running up his credit cards like there is no tomorrow. Then he comes to you and tells you that he's having trouble keeping up with the interest on his credit cards and so could he please take more of your allowance to pay his interest, so he doesn't have to beat your ass. You agree. Next, he comes to you and tells you he is going to take more of your allowance or he'll beat your ass, but for this one he promises to give you an allowance when you get old. You agree, intent on avoiding having your ass beaten.

Then you take a job mowing lawns and your brother takes his 'share' of that new source of money and for the first time in 25 years, big brother actually has extra money. You say, "Hey big brother, how about giving me back some of that money, or at least using it to pay down your credit cards."

Big Brother laughs at you.

Now you understand the Surplus. So let's get back to that Bait of the Union Address.

Back to the Bait of the Union Address

So you've got this HUGE pile of other peoples money (a "Surplus") and you really want them all to cut you some slack for High Crimes and Misdemeanors. So it's time to roll out the barrel, open the wine and *cut the cheese* cause this party is gonna rock. But damn, you're just a boy from Arkansas, how you gonna figure out all these here ciphers? Heck, some of em got more zeros than you've had bimbos. Sure you learnt your sums in school, but it would be a lot easier if you could just get all this here money in perspective. I mean, how much is a lot when you're cutting up a few trillion?

Ok . . . . calm down. We'll just do it like we were budgeting our own paycheck back in Arkansas. That'll make it easy. Here's how Billy Jeff did it:

Bill Clinton's Budgeting Key
Budget Surplus = $70 Bill.

Expense Item	Pct.	US Budget Equiv.
Car Payment	60%	$42 Billion
Trailer House Pmt.	16%	$11.2 Billion
Gas Money	5%	Bout $4 Billion
Gifts for dames	5%	Bout $4 Billion
Allowance-Hillary	1%	Call it a Billion
Pork Rinds	2%	$2 Billion
Beer	5%	Bout $4 Billion
McDonalds	1%	Call it a Billion
Donuts	1%	Call it a Billion
Diet Pepsi	1%	Call it a Billion
Church Donations	0%	Ahh, ferget it.
Donuts w/ sprinkles	2%	$2 Billion
Diet Coke	1%	Call it a Billion
Them good crescent rolls from France	1%	Call it a Billion
Titty Bar tips	5%	Bout $4 Billion
Total	106%	Bout $79 Billion

We went over budget a little bit but that's what those credit cards are for. So now B.J. Clinton can now sit down and finish that speech.

The Bait of the Union Address included the following freebies. I've indicated the Catch O' the Day for each of the pretty lures listed:

The Bait
A government board to direct investment of some Social Security funds into Private Investments.
The Catch O' the Day
Wall Street, those concerned about Social Security who are also Fools, Baby Boomers, Bureaucrats, and Lawyers.

The Bait
A new pension plan subsidized by Washington to supplement Social Security.
The Catch O' the Day
Wall Street, Baby Boomers, Pension Plan Administrators of America, and Lawyers.

The Bait
$1000 tax credits for long term health care.
The Catch O' the Day
Health Care Industry, Children with Parents, Tax Cheats, and Lawyers.

The Bait
A tripling of funding for federal summer school and after school programs.
The Catch O' the Day
Children's Program. Under current regulations, must be supported by everyone except Nazis and homophobes.

The Bait
$200 million to 'turn around' failing schools.
The Catch O' the Day
Children's Program. Under current regulations, must be
supported by everyone except Nazis and homophobes.

The Bait
New Federal resources to help teachers 'reach higher
standards'.
The Catch O' the Day
Children's Program. Under current regulations, must be
supported by everyone except Nazis and homophobes.
Specifically benefits persons involved in "Teacher
Standards' scams.

The Bait
A six-fold increase in college scholarships for students
who commit to teach in impoverished areas.
The Catch O' the Day
People who live in impoverished areas and gun shop owners
and cell phone dealers who will sell guns and cell phones to
teachers who must commute to impoverished areas.

The Bait
Federal funding to increase funding for federal charter
schools.
The Catch O' the Day
Children's Program. Under current regulations, must be
supported by everyone except Nazis and homophobes. Also
benefits the administrators and employees of the federal
charter schools, whatever the hell those are.

The Bait
Federal Funding to help communities to 'build or modernize' 5000 schools.

The Catch O' the Day
Children's Program. Under current regulations, must be supported by everyone except Nazis and homophobes. Also benefits contractors specializing in 'building or modernizing school' scams.

The Bait
A $1 minimum wage increase.

The Catch O' the Day
Minimum wage earners, which vastly outnumber minimum wage payers in the polls.

The Bait
More money for bureaucracies that enforce equal pay issues.

The Catch O' the Day
Minimum wage earners and bureaucrats and lawyers who enforce equal pay issues, all of which vastly outnumber wage payers in the polls.

The Bait
Tax credits and subsidies for child care.

The Catch O' the Day
The Child Care industry, working parents, parents not presently working who will need to when the stock market takes a nice healthy correction, Tax Cheats.

The Bait
Tax credits for stay-at-home parents.
The Catch O' the Day
Stay at home parents, until the stock market takes a nice healthy correction, forcing them back into the workplace, Tax Cheats.

The Bait
Expansion of the family leave laws to cover small companies
The Catch O' the Day
Employees of small companies, who vastly outnumber owners of small companies in the polls, and Lawyers.

The Bait
Federal regulations prohibiting the refusal to promote workers with children.
The Catch O' the Day
Huh? I didn't realize this was a problem. May be in the works as 'prophylactic' legislation. Just in case anybody ever does do this. Even if nobody ever does it Lawyers and Bureaucrats will benefit.

The Bait
More regulations governing medical care.
The Catch O' the Day
Government Bureaucrats involved in the regulation of Health Care, who in the polls vastly outnumber the number of individuals involved in providing or receiving health care. Also Lawyers.

The Bait
Make it 'easier' for small businesses to offer health care.
The Catch O' the Day
Here's your bone, small business owners. What with the 'more regulations' governing medical care, the 'expansion of family leave laws' to cover your employees and the '$1 increase in the minimum wage', you *will* need it.

The Bait
A reduction in the Medicare eligibility age from 65 to 55.
The Catch O' the Day
All those under age 65 who are incapable of understanding that the cost of Medicare is already killing us, who vastly outnumber in the polls those capable of understanding it.

The Bait
Regulations to allow people with disabilities to keep their government health insurance if they go to work.
The Catch O' the Day
People with both Disabilities and Government Health Insurance.

The Bait
A 'down payment' to federally subsidize additional medical care for the poor.
The Catch O' the Day
The Health Care Industry and The Poor. What's this 'down payment' business? You make a 'down payment' when you buy something *really* expensive, right? What did we buy?

The Bait
More federal money for mental illness issues.
The Catch O' the Day
Sufferers of mental health problems, like 'Post Dramatic Stress Syndrome', for example.

The Bait
Federal lawsuits against tobacco companies, the loot going to Medicare.
The Catch O' the Day
Everyone except "Bastard Nazi Tobacco" companies.

The Bait
More money to "enable workers to get a skills grant to choose the training they need."
The Catch O' the Day
All those minimum wage earners yearning for a sabbatical from slingin' burgers and all those unemployed and welfare folks who need a little more time before getting their butts back to work.

The Bait
A "dramatic increase in federal support for adult literacy."
The Catch O' the Day
All those unopposed to Adult Literacy. Special emphasis will be given to the oft-misunderstood words 'is' and 'alone'.

The Bait
Money to move more people off welfare.
The Catch O' the Day
Everyone but those ON welfare.

The Bait
More federal support for "community development banks."
The Catch O' the Day
The customers and employees of "community development banks." (Community Development Banks are the banks the government set up to loan money to people and businesses that never intend to pay it back. This was needed to correct discrimination, by banks that preferred to be repaid, against people and businesses that wanted to borrow money with no intention to pay it back.)

The Bait
More federal support for "empowerment zones."
The Catch O' the Day
Those who favor "empowerment zones." Whatever the hell those are. Probably something to do with self-esteem or psychic vortexes.

The Bait
100,000 more federal housing vouchers.
The Catch O' the Day
100,000 people who are guaranteed to support one each Impeached President.

The Bait
A federal program to "help businesses raise up to $15 billion to bring jobs to the inner city."
The Catch O' the Day
Businesses presently involved or potentially involved in 'inner city job' scams.

The Bait
More federal "crop insurance."
The Catch O' the Day
Unlucky Farmers.

The Bait
More federal "farm income assistance."
The Catch O' the Day
Farmers who farm poorly or not at all.

The Bait
A 28% increase in "long-term computing research."
The Catch O' the Day
All those who grasp the impact of computers on society and the profound effect that government has had on advancing computer science. An example would be the 1998 government study that revealed you could see dirty pictures if you got a modem. That study prompted Executive Order Number 324, "Emergency Government Modem Purchase Authorization."

The Bait
More U.S. taxpayer support for "economic growth abroad."
The Catch O' the Day
This one stumped me for a minute. How could he be buying votes with this? Then it hit me. (Hint: 'Buddhist Temples')

The Bait
Loan Guarantees to "American manufacturers hit hard" by the Asian economic crisis.
The Catch O' the Day
American manufacturers hit hard by the Asian crisis who make significant contributions to the Party of the President, also certain Buddhist Temples.

The Bait
Money to beef up security at American Embassies.
The Catch O' the Day
Everyone but Ossama Bin Laden. (Why don't we just kill the bastard? I know it's against the law, but it's not like we'd *impeach* the President for doing it or lying about it. In a pinch the President could confess to having a private consensual sexual relationship with Ossama Bin Laden. Then it would be *clearly* Ok.)

The Bait
More money to "prepare local communities for biological and chemical emergencies."
The Catch O' the Day
Primarily benefits the Body Bag Manufacturers of America.

The Bait
More money to "support research into vaccines and treatments" stemming from biological or chemical terrorism.
The Catch O' the Day
Those involved in 'biological or chemical terrorism vaccines and treatment' scams.

The Bait
More money to help restrain the spread of nuclear missiles.
The Catch O' the Day
Everyone but Ossama Bin Laden and others hoping to obtain nuclear missiles that have not yet made substantial contributions to a presidential election campaign like the Chinese.

The Bait
More money for military readiness and modernization.
The Catch O' the Day
The military, and realists.

The Bait
More money for military pay.
The Catch O' the Day
The military, and realists. This pay increase is necessary because potential soldiers must be willing to take lower benefits in the military than under the 'AmeriCorps' paid volunteer program. (This is in addition to risking getting killed, of course.) The new GI bill awards total potential

education benefits of $7,316 for a six-year military
service commitment. This compares to benefits of $4,725
for one year of 'volunteer' service under the AmeriCorps
program. In addition, AmeriCorps 'volunteers' don't risk
jail and a dishonorable discharge for lying or for
consensual sex like soldiers do. As a result, they don't
face the ethical quandary faced by military service
personnel in serving under a dishonored Commander in
Chief.

The Bait
More money for the United Nations.
The Catch O' the Day
Friends of the Psychic Network.

The Bait
The creation of "Radio Democracy for Africa."
The Catch O' the Day
The bored and underemployed employees of "Radio Free
Europe".

The Bait
Taxpayer support for the "African Trade and Development
Act."
The Catch O' the Day
Apparently we are now enacting legislation for entire
continents. Some continents suffer for a lack of adequate
government regulation and this begins the process of
exporting part of our surplus government regulation. Chief
beneficiary: participants in 'African Trade and
Development' scams.

The Bait
Money for 50,000 more police officers.
The Catch O' the Day
The Law Enforcement Industry and The Donut Industry.

The Bait
Money to equip the police with "new tools, from crime-mapping computers to digital mug shots."
The Catch O' the Day
The Law Enforcement Industry. (New get-tough freeway signage: "Commit a Crime, Get a Web Page.")

The Bait
More money for drug testing and treatment.
The Catch O' the Day
The Law Enforcement Industry, The Drug Testing Industry, The Drug Treatment Industry. (New freeway signage: "Don't do Drugs, Or Urine Trouble.")

The Bait
Additional regulations on gun ownership.
The Catch O' the Day
Government Bureaucrats and those who haven't figured out the low violent crime rates enjoyed by states that facilitate responsible gun ownership.

The Bait
More regulations on gun manufacturers.
The Catch O' the Day
Government Bureaucrats and those who haven't figured out the low violent crime rates enjoyed by states that facilitate responsible gun ownership.

The Bait
More money for the "Safe and Drug Free School Act."
The Catch O' the Day
Everyone unfortunate enough to have their kids in public schools because they don't care about their children or don't know any better or can't afford private schools because all their money is eaten up in taxes.

The Bait
New federal "clean air fund."
The Catch O' the Day
Eco-Nazis, and a new crop of Bureaucrats.

The Bait
Tax incentives and federal investment "to spur clean energy technologies."
The Catch O' the Day
Tax cheats and Clean Energy Technologies scam artists.

The Bait
A $1 billion "Livability Agenda" to combat urban sprawl.
The Catch O' the Day
'Livability' scam artists, like Al Gore.

The Bait
A $1 billion "Lands Legacy Initiative" to preserve places of natural beauty.
The Catch O' the Day
Earth Firsters and a fair number of wealthy owners of otherwise worthless land who would like to get in on splitting up a billion bucks.

The Bait
More federal funding for AmeriCorps.
The Catch O' the Day
Present and future unskilled AmeriCorps employees who prefer government work to flipping burgers, even at a dollar an hour more. ('AmeriCorps' is the volunteerism program initiated by the Clinton administration. Volunteers have always been understood to be unpaid by the very definition of the word. The AmeriCorps program redefines this for us. But they don't call it pay, they call it a 'living allowance'. When your parents quit giving you an allowance the government will, under this program.) When you understand this program you understand America's shrinking welfare rolls. We've just renamed it.

The Bait
Money to fund a "Employment Nondiscrimination Act and the Hate Crimes Prevention Act."
The Catch O' the Day
Anyone who can dream up a way to include themselves in a minority classification and thereby win greater government protections and benefits than non-minority-classified citizens.

The Bait
More money to "significantly expand" efforts to help
immigrants learn English and American history.
The Catch O' the Day
Special emphasis will be given to the words 'is' and 'alone'.
The additional funds will also allow expanded coverage of
the sexual peccadilloes of former Presidents and any
Republican Congressman.

But Wait! That's not all! The State of the Union Address
didn't include just Bait. The State of the Union Address
included vision, sentiment, and drama.

Rosa Parks was there. Little Rosa Parks, who
courageously refused to move to the back of the bus 43
years ago. Rosa Parks, who proved her courage so many
years ago, was there to provide her skirts for the
President to hide behind.

Tommy Sosa was there. Tommy Sosa, who had
provided so many Exciting Baseball Moments for America.
Tommy Sosa was there to be Hispanic and be a human
segue into promises to Hispanic voters.

Suzann Wilson, of Jonesboro, Arkansas was there.
Suzann Wilson, who had lost her daughter at the
Jonesboro tragedy, was there to provide the Impeached
President with a skirt behind which to hide another
tiresome and blatant appeal to further dilute the
Constitutional guarantee of the right to bear arms.

Captain Jeff Taliaferro, a 10-year veteran of the
Air Force was there. Captain Jeff Taliaferro, who flew a
B-1B bomber over Iraq as we attacked Saddam Hussien's
war machine in Operation Desert Fox to divert attention
from the Impeachment of the President, was there.

Captain Jeff Taliaferro was there to sit there and shut up because he was ordered by his lying puke of a Commander in Chief to be there and sit there and shut up.

And **Hillary Clinton** was there. Hillary Clinton was there to be Honored by the Impeached President. Honored for all she had done to be Honored for. Honored for her Honorable defense of her husband and the TrailerPark Presidency when she acted like she didn't even suspect he was lying. And Honored for her Honorable defense of her husband and the TrailerPark Presidency when she acted like she suspected he was lying but was trying not to believe it could be true with the Plain Fat Girl. Honored for her Honorable defense of her husband and the TrailerPark Presidency even when a semen stained dress proved her worst fears. And Honored for Honorably showing up for the State of the Union address to be used by the President one more time in spite of the fact that she looked like she had been crying for days and had about six stiff drinks before coming. "Hillary", he said, "I *honor* you." And Honor her he has. In his own special way.

The Bipartisan Phase of a Senate Trial
Part III: The Prosecution

The Senate trial was prosecuted by the "Case Managers" appointed by the Judicial Committee of the House of Representatives. Think of them as a troop of brownies showing up for a gang war. They got diced like an unarmed man in a knife fight.

It's not that they didn't have the facts on their side, they did. It's not that they didn't have the law on their side, they did. It's not that they didn't have the Constitution on their side, they did. They played by the rules. And they got their butts kicked around the block. You see; they played by the rules. Big Mistake.

The fact of the matter is that the case against the president was real, real simple. All the bullshit, analysis and posturing aside, the applicable laws are an easy read and make for one of the most straightforward cases possible. The facts are irrefutable; again, bullshit aside. So why was the prosecution constantly being put on the defensive? Real simple, folks, they made two fundamental mistakes. In **Prosecution Mistake Number One** they tried the case in front of the Senate but not in front of the American People. In **Prosecution Mistake Number Two** they failed to acknowledge it *was* about sex, and that they should have made the point forcefully. (But, to be fair, it must be noted that the PressnPolls branch of the Gov't wasn't exactly on the side of truth on this one. They are pretty good at exposing the garage mechanic who lies to you but they don't seem too interested in exposing the Government that lies to you.)

Prosecution Mistake Number One simply boils down to the fact that the prosecution never had the guts to stand up in front of a camera, and America, and call a spade a spade. Night after night America got to see the Defense get up and spew the most vacuous and specious arguments ever invented, all spun up in a web of false complexity to obfuscate the real issues. And never, ever, not even once, did the Prosecution (or the press) effectively call them out on their bullshit. This all really started in the House when the Prosecution let the Defense get away with calling them partisan again and again and again. The clear fact in the House was that, given the facts of the case and given the crossover votes of Democrats voting to impeach, the accusation of partisanship was clearly as empty as the brains and moral/ethical nerve centers of the President's defenders. But the House Managers and the Republican House members and the Republican Senators and the Press let them spew the lie night after night after night. Not once did the prosecution side rise up on their hind legs and forcefully rebut the ridiculous accusation. The House Managers should have appointed one of their number as a 'Mad Dog of Soundbites'. That member should have repeatedly and forcefully responded to each and every spin and public appeal of the Defense. Something like the following might have helped:

Issue: You guys are guilty of Partisanship!
Response: That's Bullshit. The Partisans here are the Democrats. Look at the votes.

Issue: These offenses don't "Rise to the Level of Impeachment".
Response: That's bullshit. Look at the federal sentencing guidelines on Perjury and Bribery. Perjury has **stricter** sentencing guidelines than Bribery. Arguments that the offenses don't 'rise to the level of an impeachable offense', don't rise to the level of rational thought.

Issue: It wasn't fair to vote to impeach the President in the House without calling witnesses!
Response: Bullshit. There was plenty of evidence and the WhiteHouse didn't call a single fact witness. Please stop insulting the intelligence of the Average American with vacuous lies.

Issue: We don't need witnesses in the Senate trial.
Response: Bullshit, don't even DREAM that we are going to let 45 Democrat Senators and the occasional ethics-impaired Republican violate their oath to do 'impartial justice' without making sure there is a clear and convincing record of a trial and their partiality in the face of objective facts.

Prosecution Mistake Number Two: It really *was* about sex, and the Prosecution should never have taken the Defense's bait on the issue. A statement like the following may have served to illustrate the point:

Mad Dog of Soundbites: "The issue before our Country is rooted in the behavior of Billie Jeff Clinton and no one else. Billie Jeff engaged in sexual activity with an intern in the WhiteHouse. He had the audacity to engage in sexual activity while on the phone with members of the Legislature. This President caused Ms. Lewinski to be hired onto the WhiteHouse staff from her position as intern in order to further his sexual shenanigans with her. He later assisted this woman, his paramour, in finding employment in the private sector in order to maintain good relations with her; to shut her up. He clearly encouraged her to lie about it in her deposition to the Paula Jones Federal Civil Rights Lawsuit to protect himself. Let's not forget that the Paula Jones Federal Civil Rights lawsuit was brought forward because of unwanted attempts at the same sort of sexual misbehavior this President later involved Ms. Lewinsky in. This President lied repeatedly to the American People; his staff, and even to Buddy, his dog.

This President, through his inability to control his base sexual urges, has brought dishonor to his person, to the Office of the President, and to this Nation. But we can't impeach him for that.

The simple fact is that the Founding Fathers could never have imagined such disgusting and incredibly stupid behavior on the part of a President. If they had, the Constitution of the United States would certainly have read "High Crimes and Misdemeanors and Generally Having the Judgement, Manners and Morals of an Un-Neutered Puppy Humping a Leg in a Public Place". But it doesn't, so we can't impeach him for that.

But he lied to a Federal Grand Jury. And then he attempted to Obstruct Justice. We can and should impeach him and remove him from office for that.

The facts of his sexual behavior, his lies to the American People, his staff, and his dog, Buddy, cannot be ignored and should bear heavily on this matter. The dishonor his has brought upon himself and the Office of the President render him unfit for **any** public office."

The Bipartisan Phase of a Senate Trial Part I I I I: The Defense of the TrailerPark President

B.J. Clinton's Legal Defense against Impeachment and Removal can be summarized as follows:

"Grasp at enough straws and you will soon get a pile of the same results that you would have gotten had you fed those straws to your bull"

Where to begin? I guess one could say that it depends on what the meaning of the word 'is', is. It may depend upon how you define 'alone'. Can you believe that the *President of the United States* actually expected us to swallow that load of bull? He really *doesn't* give us much credit, does he?

Spend one hour reading the relevant sections of Starr Report and the transcript of the House Impeachment hearings. Be Objective. Then say to yourself, based upon what I know of the President and given his repeated apologies to everyone in the universe for 'misleading' them, is the man guilty of lying before a Grand Jury and Obstructing Justice or not? Bingo. Case Solved. Congratulations: for you have seen the light. There is simply no defense against the fact that B.J. Clinton committed perjury and obstructed justice.

Close your eyes and remember everything you can that was said in front of the House of Representatives and the Senate in defense of the Impeached President. Imagine them giving that testimony in front of any Congress of thirty years ago or prior. Each of those defenders would have had one of two things happen to them. They would have gone to jail for contempt for bringing such specious

and idiotic arguments before Congress. Or they would
have been committed for feeblemindedness. In the
America of the TrailerPark President we were actually
expected to sit back and accept ridiculous tripe, wrapped
up in big words delivered by ethics-impaired 'experts', as
somehow relevant.

But wait! There's more! When you buy into the B.J.
Clinton SpinMaster 2000 you get more! Those of you who
call in during this program will receive not one, not two,
but THREE B.J. Clinton FallBack Defense Positions. These
B.J. Clinton FallBack Defense Positions are made of the
finest Whole Cloth and are Guaranteed, that's right
GUARANTEED to obfuscate the true issues and permit
B.J.'s mouthpieces to blow smoke.

B.J. Clinton's Fallback Defense Positions

You are gonna love this. OK, understand that B.J. was
Impeached. The House voted and that was a done puppy.
So pretend we are now in the middle of the Senate trial.
The Senate trial, under the Constitution, was held to
determine if B.J. Clinton was guilty of the "High Crimes
and Misdemeanors" that the House impeached him for.
The questions become: "Did B.J. Clinton commit Perjury
before the Grand Jury?" and, "Did B.J. Clinton Obstruct
Justice?"

If the answer to *either* one is yes, then B.J. Clinton is
convicted and must be removed from office under Article
I, Section 4 of the Constitution. That is that. No way
around it. It does not and should not matter whether you
like the guy or his policies or not. It does not and should

not matter that you belong to one political party or
another.

If you actually looked at the transcript you know what
should have happened. (You may come to a different
conclusion if you stick your head up your ass while
reviewing the documentation. Try it. Read it once and
write down your answer. Then stick your head up your ass
and read it again. Write down your answer. See? It
makes a big difference.)

Fallback Position Number One
'If the level's not so high, you must let my client fly'
B.J. Clinton wanted you to believe that the Senators
were also to determine if the crimes 'rise to the level of
removable offenses'. That's a new phrase in the history of
the known universe so lets say it all together one time.
"Rise to the Level of Removable Offenses." Really does
have a smart, educated sound to it, doesn't it? But let me
ask you this. Did you notice an aftertaste after you said
it? Do you remember what you get when you grasp at too
many straws? Yep.   Pure Bull. Just don't you swallow it.

Nothing about that phrase in the Constitution. In
actuality, the phrase did not exist until B.J. Clinton's team
dreamt it up. It's kind of an evolution of the phrase; 'Rise
to the Level of an Impeachable Offense' which died when
B.J. Clinton was Impeached.

I'm just here to tell you that I, for one, am mighty glad
that neither phrase has the word 'is' or 'alone' in it. Can
you imagine that? The B.J. Clinton Crack Legal Defense
Think Tank would have had a *field* day with that.

Hiraldo Riviera: "We're talking with Mr. Alan
Lackowitz, Professor of Law at the Convoluted
School of Law. Alan, what happens now that the
nation has awakened to the fact that the 'Crimes
Don't Rise to the Level of a Removable Offense'
argument makes no sense whatsoever under the
Constitution and is clearly a meaningless
construction of the Impeached President's Crack
Legal Defense Think Tank?"

Alan Lackowitz: "Well Hiraldo, then the question
clearly becomes do the crimes 'rise is to the level
alone of removable offenses'. The Impeached
President has already testified to the fact that he
is unclear as to the meanings of either the word 'is'
or the word 'alone'. How could he be removed in the
face of such ambiguity? It wouldn't be fair,
Hiraldo, it just wouldn't be fair. I know about being
a persecuted victim, Peter. I wallow in it and I've
exploited it my whole life. Trust me on this, it
would not be fair. And trust me, Hiraldo, we aren't
done coming up with memorable rhymes in defense
of this president."

Hiraldo Riviera: "Well, I guess we can take your
word on that, Professor Lackowitz. Polls indicate
that over 90% of Americans do not understand the
phrase 'rise is to the level alone of removable
offenses'. The Impeached President may be able
to avoid removal from office if at least 50
Senators don't understand it either. Just as in
your defense of the innocent and wrongfully
accused and victimized O.J. Simpson and Mike

Tyson, you and your team have crafted a masterful
and gutsy defense."

Alan Lackowitz: "Thanks Hiraldo, speaking of gutsy,
you know I like to go to nude beaches don't you?

Hiraldo Riviera: "Cool"

Alan Lackowitz: "It takes guts for a guy with a
body like mine to stroll down a beach naked,
Hiraldo, real guts. I'm a gutsy guy. I've got chutzpa.
In fact, I wrote the book on it."

Hiraldo Riviera: "Cool Alan, maybe I can come with
you to a nude beach sometime and we can 'hang out'
together."

(Alan and Hiraldo start tittering so badly that
Hiraldo has to break for a commercial message.)

Fallback Position Number Two
*'If he lied 'bout getting ass, you must let my client
pass'*

Alan LackoWitz, Expert Witness for the President:
"The Founding Fathers never envisioned a President being
impeached for lying about sex. The Founding Fathers
wrote that Article of the Constitution to enable a
President to be removed for acts that were 'High Crimes
and Misdemeanors', and clearly didn't mean lying about sex.
John Madison, at the Constitutional convention in 1787,
spoke of the need for impeachment as a way to defend the
nation against "the incapacity, negligence or perfidy" of a
president. In the Federalist Papers, Alexander Hamilton
referred to "the misconduct of public men, or... the abuse
or violation of some public trust." John Madison and
Alexander Hamilton certainly would never have foreseen

the Impeachment clause being used against a President who gets blowjobs in the oval office from a youthful intern while talking on the phone to congressmen. Could they? No, I think it's safe to say that James Madison and Alexander Hamilton could never have even imagined it. See? So they could NOT have meant "High Crimes and Misdemeanors and Blowjobs in the Office or Lying about Blowjobs in the Office". They were smart men. If they had meant to say that then they certainly would have. It is clear, by their silence on the issue, that while the Founding Fathers may not have approved of getting blowjobs in the office while on the phone to Congresspersons and then lying about it and trying to cover it up, they certainly didn't consider it impeachable.

Only a racist or homophobe could disagree.

I rest this part of my case."

Fallback Position Number Three
> *'My client's guilt is plain as sin, but I will die before I let you win'*

The Impeached President, his desperate back against the wall, calls on his defense team to burn their boats. There is no going back. Operation 'Crazy MAD' is unleashed upon the Congress and the People of the United States. It's a three pronged campaign to the last liberal:

Operation Crazy MAD

Crazy, as in insane. MAD, as in Mutually Assured Destruction.

We turn now to Mr. Charlie RuffnPuff, latest in a long, long string of lawyers defending the Impeached President, on the floor of the Senate:

"Mr. Chief Justice, members of the Senate, distinguished managers: William Jefferson Clinton is guilty of the charges that have been preferred against him. He did commit perjury. He did obstruct justice. He must **not** be removed from office.

Now, merely to say those words brings into sharp relief the fact that I and my colleagues are here today, in this great chamber defending the President of the United States against all logic and common sense.

We seek on his behalf no more than we know you will give us — a fair opportunity to be heard, a fair assessment of this latest argument we have come up with, and a one time pass on High Crimes and Misdemeanors.

We will not defend the president on the facts and on the law and on the constitutional principles that must guide your deliberations. Some have suggested that we do so. We do not. Instead we come before you today with Excuses, Threats, and a Way Out. Excuses, Threats, and a Way Out.

Excuses
No one can defend William Jefferson Clinton before you today; but we can pity him. The Impeached President is a victim. No less that the Blacks and Jews or Women or Gays. By all that is Holy and embodied in Christmas, and Hanukah, and Kwanzaa, and yes, Ramadan; the Impeached President is a victim. Respected Senators, William

Jefferson Clinton is innocent by reason of INSANITY, but NOT the kind of insanity that means you would have to remove him from office for being insane."

(At this point the proceedings were interrupted by high-pitched whine of overheating zoom lenses as cameras were panned throughout the Chamber to gauge the reaction to this revelation. There was almost no reaction whatsoever, except for an eye-rolling 'wave' executed by Senate Republicans. The Chamber was quickly brought to order.)

"Several Medical Professionals, trained to work in a doctor's world, have been fully prepared to appear before you and testify that the Impeached President is and has been suffering from severe Post Dramatic Stress Syndrome. Only with recent advances in science was his condition able to be created....ahh, strike that,...... ah, diagnosed. Post Dramatic Stress Syndrome is brought about by being conflicted and in denial and constantly under the strain of having to dramatically lie about things to protect people you really love and are committed to, like a wife or daughter and the American People. Only to protect them, never for yourself. Imagine it Senators, if you can. Please try. Imagine the horror of it. It would be enough to drive any man caught getting blowjobs in his office from an employee during working hours and on the phone to Congressmen, INSANE! Imagine the horror.

Further, these Medical Professionals are prepared to testify that the Impeached President's insanity, although severe enough to warrant being a defense against Perjury and Obstruction of Justice, does **not** rise to the level of insanity necessary to warrant your removing him from office for insanity."

(At this point, the proceedings were interrupted while the Chief Justice cautioned Senator Tom Barkin that he was not permitted to 'Whoop' or 'High Five' during the trial.)

"They are prepared to testify for days and weeks on end! Yes, honorable Senators, they are prepared to testify till the cows.. come.. home."

(At this point, the proceedings were again interrupted while the Chief Justice ordered the Sergeant at Arms to remove Senator Tom Barkin from the Chamber for 'Whooping' again.)

Additionally, honorable Senators who are not jurors and should not ever be referred to as such, the President's behavior in this matter was only in the National Interest. As you are aware, Ms. Monica Lewinsky testified that the president told her, and I quote the Starr Report now, that "she and the President had a lengthy conversation that day. He told her that he suspected that a foreign embassy (he did not specify which one) was tapping his telephones, and he proposed cover stories. If ever questioned, she should say that the two of them were just friends. If anyone ever asked about their phone sex, she should say that they knew their calls were being monitored all along, and the phone sex was just a put-on."

You see, gentle and understanding and forgiving Senators, the President was only fighting the forces of an insidious plot by a foreign embassy, or maybe some drug guys, when he engaged in what may have appeared to have been a selfish and tacky sexual relationship with Monica Lewinsky. A plot so evil, so insidious, that he could reveal it to no one, not even to a Federal Grand Jury. He did this not for himself, but in service to the American People. He discovered this plot on his own, and he believed this plot was so evil and dangerous that the CIA had not even briefed **him** about it. And you know how those CIA guys are, especially those of you who serve on the Senate Secret Plots Committee. Those guys would just as soon kill you as look at you, I kid you not.

So this President, in a brave and selfless sacrifice to the American People, engaged in a sexual liaison, deriving no pleasure from it, let me assure you; and then fibbed but did not commit perjury before a Grand Jury, and did other things which stopped just short of rising to Impeachable Offenses, in order to draw out the enemies of Democracy. If necessary, we will call on none other than Hillary Clinton, the First Lady, who will testify that he told her similar stories of plots of foreign embassies, or drug guys.

So I beg you, kind and honorable Senators, to set aside these charges that were, after all, brought up to you by the Partisan Witches' Brew Brewing, Dung Heap Heaping, House of Representatives Partisan Evil Empire. And forget, with me, that some democrats voted to impeach him too.
But wait! Honorable Senators, that's not all!

Threats
You are no doubt aware of the wave of Politics of Personal Destruction that threatens the Republicans, ah...strike that; the Republic. You know, from his public speeches, that our Impeached President abhors this threat and has, already, appointed a Committee Revolting

Against the Politics of Personal Destruction, also known as
CRAPPD. This President, our President, nay; your
President, is prepared to pledge to you that if you acquit
him, he will stop at nothing, that's right, nothing, to find
the perpetrators of this insidious threat and bring them
to justice. Only this President, this man, can stop this
threat in its tracks. I know you understand what I mean
by that. If you remove this President, he cannot continue
to lead and work with CRAPPD, and you know what that
means. Don't you, Senators? The Political Earth will be
scorched. Somewhere in this country, behind some veil of
secrecy, behind some curtain, hides a veritable WIZARD
of the Politics of Personal Destruction. He may never be
found, he may never come out from behind the curtain of
secrecy but this President has a pretty good idea who he
is and pledges to you that he will be stopped if you acquit
him. The President I mean. Acquit the President.

Further, kind Senators who are not jurors but
nonetheless not to be tampered with, it is clear that the
President must be allowed to present his defense. That
would only be fair and the President has never asked for
anything but fairness and thinks you should be fair. You
cannot let this be a 'Rush to Judgement' like the rush to
judgement that almost resulted in a guilty verdict in the
wrongful trial of one of America's greatest sports heroes
a couple of years ago. Do you remember that trial, gentle
Senators? That trial lasted over six months and there was
no small concern that there would be **race riots** if a guilty
verdict was found. Six months and that was a clear rush to
judgement. So if that trial took six months and was almost
a rush to judgement, how much time might be appropriate

to avoid making this one a rush to judgement? A year? Two years? Who can say?

So, given that and the fact that the Impeached President currently enjoys the highest approval rating in the history of the universe, you know what you need to do, don't you, Senators?

But wait! That's not all!

A Way Out

You all swore an oath to do impartial justice in this proceeding. Each of you, setting party affiliations aside, are pledged to do just that. To render impartial justice and uphold the Constitution. And I can tell you no one is more supportive of that than our Impeached President. To do less; would bring dishonor.

Your oath was clear. ``I solemnly swear that in all things appertaining to the trial of the impeachment of William Jefferson Clinton, now pending, I will do impartial justice according to the Constitution and laws: So help me God.''

A crystal clear oath, Gentlepersons. And given the facts of this case, the law, and the Constitution, your duty is clear. Virtually all reasonable persons, and many small pets, know that President William Jefferson Clinton is guilty, guilty guilty. It seems that you must to convict this President to properly discharge your oath. Some of you are prepared to vote that way without regard to the public opinion polls the founding fathers thoughtlessly left out of the Constitution. A crystal clear oath....

But is it? Look at it again.

"I solemnly swear that in all things appertaining to the trial of the impeachment of William Jefferson Clinton, now pending, I will do impartial justice according to the Constitution and laws: So help me God.''

The meaning of this oath depends on the meaning of **words**, kind Senators. Words.

Words with meanings subject to definition. Words with definitions subject to different meanings. Do you see where I'm going with this? I see many of you nodding. Good. You see it. For those of you having difficulty seeing my point, just let me say that the oath doesn't contain the words 'is' or 'alone', does it? But it contains lots of other words. It contains words as easily misunderstood, as 'is', and 'alone', doesn't it?

Look at the oath, Senators. I mean, it's got words like 'swear' and 'impartial' and 'justice' and 'according'. Hell, one of em's got a suffix, fer Christ's sake! The words 'is' and 'alone' are pieces of **cake** compared to these words.

Who among you cannot say you have not misunderstood a word? Who among you could not interpret that oath the same way that virtually all Democrat Congresspersons interpret it? To do so would be BIPARTISAN, kind Senators.

I rest my case for the Bipartisan Phase of the Senate Trial, and I thank you, kind Senators who are not jurors and not to be tampered with, for your time and attention. I am confident that you will make the right decisions for you are now armed with the all the Excuses, Threats and Ways Out, necessary to render impartial justice."

The Bipartisan Phase of the Senate Trial Part IIIII: The Papal Visit

According to the Senate Impeachment Trial Rules both the Prosecution and Defense were entitled to Religious Representation. The Prosecution having called Pat Robertson, the Impeached President called on Gods Own Representative on Earth. Pope John Paul II met with the Impeached President, and the Impeached President's attorneys, in St. Louis on Jan 26, 1999.

The meeting began, awkwardly, with the men greeting. When the Pope began waving his hand in the sign of the cross, the President grabbed the Pope's hand in the mistaken belief that the Pope wanted to do a 'brother shake'. Their meeting was then interrupted twice. First when the Pope had to be restrained for 'slapping' at the President, and a second time when the Pope collapsed.

St. Louis, Missouri: Pope John Paul II collapsed today while meeting with the impeached President of the United States. The Pope was rushed to the nearest medical facility, the 'William Jefferson Clinton Family Planning and Abortion QuickMart', where his condition quickly worsened. Finally, after being medivac'ed to 'Our Mother of Mercy, Save Us From That Godless, Witless Bastard of a President' hospital, Pope John Paul II was stabilized and is now listed in "About the President, but not publicly of course, very critical" condition. Apparently Pope John Paul II's collapse occurred just as the impeached President was asking the Pope if he would hear his confession. White House spokesman Joe 'Curt' Lockhart, when asked about the Pope's collapse, stated: "<blink>You know the rules<blink>, you can ask the President's attorneys<blink>, we can't comment on an ongoing investigation<blink>, if you'd listen to the answer I gave earlier you would know that<blink>, I won't amplify on the clear statements of the President on that matter<blink>, wadda you think I am, the answer man?<blink>".

After their meeting, the White House and the Papacy issued a joint press release in which Pole John Paul II and the Impeached President of the United States jointly condemned the evils of exploitative capitalism, the Politics of Personal Destruction and euthanasia, but agreed to disagree on abortion, lying, obstruction of justice, moral responsibility, and marital fidelity.

The Impeached President announced in a humble statement the same day that he was "*A Living Apostle of Progress and Hope*". The Apostle then ordered the building of a pyramid "bigger than that one in Egypt" to be dedicated to "Progress and Hope." He said, "Let this Presidency be remembered for the fact that I have made the biggest erection of any President; ever. Let this erection, the Memorial of Progress and Hope, stand forever as a Legacy to my Presidency."

He further directed the White House Office of Protocol that, henceforth, no one would be allowed in his presence wearing a hat that made him or her taller than the President.

And to think it all began in Hope.

The Bipartisan Phase of a Senate Trial Part I I I I I I: Second Secret Senate Meeting

The Second Secret Senate Meeting was convened to consider the question of whether or not to dismiss the trial or hear witnesses. (Senators are not named to preserve the anonymity of the meeting):

> **Senator of the Evil Empire**: "We'll call the meeting together, Sergeant at Arms, have the doors been sealed and has the room been cleared?"
>
> **Sergeant at Arms**: "Yes, the room is secure, Sir."
>
> **Senator of the Evil Empire**: "Ok, listen up, this is where we're at. The President is Guilty and every one of us and the American People know it. The Polls have shaped up with virtually all non-Clue-impaired American Citizens believing him guilty but, weirdly, 80% wanting to keep him in office. You Democrats don't know whether to shit or go blind cause if we hold a vote on impeachment you will be on record as violating your oath to render impartial judgement under the Constitution. We Republicans don't know whether to shit or go blind cause if we actually impeach his ass as we know we should we stand a good chance of getting toasted in the next election. Does that about sum it up or do we need to talk about it?"
>
> **Caring Senator**: "Sounds good to me, Trent. I know I speak for my party when I say that your assessment that we don't know whether to shit or go blind is accurate."

(The proceedings were interrupted at this point when Senator Strom Thurmond's colostomy bag suffered its eighth annual massive overflow. Apparently Strom had enjoyed a big lunch. Several Senators, in a spirited display of bipartisanship, were actually forced 'across the aisle' to avoid the deluge.)

Senator of the Evil Empire: "Ok then, since we've got the votes here's how we'll play it. Me and my guys are gonna vote down the motion to dismiss the trial. If we give it up now we'll look like total jerks to the democrats and like wimps to our republican voters. The House Managers want sixty-seven witnesses but we'll give them three witnesses and that's going to be approved, again, cause we have the votes."

Caring Senator: "Whatever, Trent, just wait till we get the votes."

Senator of the Evil Empire: "All in favor?"

100 Senators: "Aye"

Senator of the Evil Empire: "Fine, Mr. Secretary, please record the votes as I've outlined. Any of you that want to cross party lines let the Secretary know."

Caring Senator: "That's great, but what about the time?"

Senator of the Evil Empire: "What do you mean, Tom?"

Caring Senator: "We said each Senator would get 5 minutes to debate, that's 500 minutes, we can't walk out of here now! The press would toast our butts."

Senator of the Evil Empire: "Yeah, ok..how's this, we'll look at those slides of Monica's thong again."
Caring Senator: "Great, but I have an idea, let's also read the deposition transcripts again. We'll do Monica in the voice of 'Scarlet' from 'Gone with the Wind!"
Senator of the Evil Empire: "Good thinking, let's say four hours and then we can adjourn. All in favor?"
100 Senators: "Aye."

Four hours later the Senate, in a tactful and collegial show of partisan decorum, left the Chamber and rushed for the 'stakeout' cameras liberally sprinkled around the Hill. The young and wiry little bastard Senator Tom Phashionable led the Democrat scrum that made it first.

Senator Tom Phashionable: "Boy are we pissed. This partisanship sucks. The Senate Republicans just ignored us and in a show of incredible partisanship voted down our bipartisan motion to dismiss the trial and approved the partisan House witness list. I think it's safe to say the Bipartisan Phase of this Trial is over."
Newsperson: "Senator, we understand a democrat voted with them, how can you call it Republican partisanship when one of your own voted with them?"
Senator Tom Phashionable: "He just got confused. You see this is all very confusing. He misunderstood the polls and the will of the American People. A group of our people has locked

him in his office and are in there now working to de-program him."

Newsperson: "Senator, now that the witness list requested by the House Managers has been approved, what can we expect?"

Senator Tom Phashionable: "The Senate will now need to develop rules for the questioning of these witnesses. Of course those rules must be fair to the WhiteHouse and bring this matter to a speedy conclusion."

Newsperson: "So we can expect to see these witnesses testifying in the well of the Senate?"

Senator Tom Phashionable: "No way. We must preserve the tactful collegial decorum of the Senate. Hearing witnesses testify on the behavior of the President would certainly not be tactful or decorous nor would it be in keeping with our reputation for either tact or decorum, and could impair our collegiality. We will propose that the witnesses be interviewed in private, no more than three minutes of testimony for each, and that summaries of their testimony be prepared by the Senate Committee on Tact, chaired by my good friend Senator Tom Barkin, and then entered into the record in sealed envelopes."

Newsperson: "Do you think that has a snowball's chance in hell of passing, given the fact that the Senate Republicans, and a Democrat, seem comfortable ignoring you?"

Senator Tom Phashionable: "Our proposals are not about passing. Our proposals are intended to show the American People that we listen to the Polls, that we want to get this over without listening to any bothersome testimony as to the facts and evidence that would only serve to hide the real issue. The real issue is that this trial is effectively over. We just voted unanimously, if you ignore all the Republicans and one Democrat, to end this trial. We are not going to let any facts or evidence get in the way of our voting. We took an oath to render impartial justice. Have you looked up "impartial?" Nothing in the definition of the word 'impartial' that says you have to consider facts or evidence. In fact, looking at facts or evidence could impair my ability to be impartial. Right now I am impartial. Examining facts could cause me to be partial. I'm simply not willing to risk it. So this trial is really over.

Newsperson: "Senator, in the Impeachment trial of Walter Nixon, a federal judge, you said, "...[He] took an oath to tell the truth and the whole truth. As a grand jury witness, it was not for him to decide what would be material. That was for the grand jury to decide. Of all people, Federal Judge Walter Nixon certainly knew this.

So I am going to vote 'guilty'... He misled the grand jury. These acts are indisputably criminal and warrant impeachment." How can you explain your vote to dismiss this trial in light of that statement?"

Senator Tom Phashionable: "I resent your implying that this President lied to a Grand Jury. In this country we believe persons are innocent until proven guilty. The President can't be guilty unless and until a verdict is rendered finding him guilty. The trial isn't over, so he's not guilty. Since it is clear he is not guilty, we should dismiss the trial. So clearly this trial is effectively over. Since the trial is effectively over and the President has not been found guilty then the not guiltiness of the President cannot be called into question."

Newsperson: "But Senator, recent polls suggest that over 70 percent of all Americans believe the President did lie under oath and did obstruct justice."

Senator Tom Phashionable: "We are tactful men of honor. We have taken an oath before God to render impartial justice. We will not be swayed by public opinion polls. Thank you."

The following morning a Major Washington Newspaper erroneously reported the following headline:

House Trial Managers Quit
"This is Bullshit", says Henry Hyde

And the President's Attorney responded to reporter's questions in a press conference:

David Spindoc: "This latest insensitive action on the part of the Senate Republicans simply illustrates their incredible uppityness. Calling witnesses is a huge mistake and a waste of time. The House didn't call witnesses in the House

Impeachment hearings, so clearly they are not necessary or appropriate. It's ridiculous to call them now."

Newsperson: "Mr. Spindoc, doesn't the fact that the House did, after all, Impeach the President indicate that they didn't **need** to call witnesses. Doesn't that seem to indicate that perhaps you were stupid not to call any fact witnesses yourself? You were, after all, rather verbose in implying you had fact witnesses that would clear the President."

David Spindoc: "I'm sorry, I couldn't hear you, next question."

Newsperson2: "How will the WhiteHouse react to these latest developments?"

David Spindoc: "If they get to call witnesses then we are going to call witnesses. They get three so we should get three.

First, we will call Pope John Paul II. The Pope will testify, at length, on forgiveness. He will testify that, during his meeting with the Apostle of Progress and Hope, that the Apostle told the Pope he was really sorry about this. He will testify that even though he believes the President to be a habitual and incorrigible liar, he believed that the President actually appeared to seem to believe himself. According to the Pope it was "the damnedest thing" he had ever seen.

Secondly, we will call Mr. Orenthal J. Simpson. Mr. Simpson will testify on fairness and false accusations. He will testify that seemingly overwhelming evidence of guilt is, in fact, not sufficient to rise to the level of guilt. He will testify that the same persons who murdered his wife could well be the perpetrators of this evil fraud upon the person of the Apostle of Progress and Hope, and may be hiding on a golf course somewhere in Florida.

Lastly, we will call the Presidents Council of Spiritual Advisors and Apologists. The Council will testify that the Apostle is really, really sorry to have said some things that could be misinterpreted as not exactly true. They will testify that the Apostle never meant, never intended, to do anything wrong; and that he only wants to do the work of the American People and really has read some parts of the bible. So there."

Newsperson2: "That will take forever, are you sure you want to do that, what with the polls saying the people want this over and all?"

David Spindoc: "Well, what we might do is wait and see what the House witnesses have to say. If they toe the line...ummmm, ahhh, I mean, tell the truth, we may just forget our witnesses and ask for an up or down vote on the articles of impeachment. This is really over, you know, because the Senate voted unanimously, if you ignore the Republicans and one Democrat, to end the trial. The WhiteHouse will also require that the witnesses just be videotaped and not appear in the well of the Senate, and that nobody can say anything bad about the President's behavior."

Newsperson2: "How can the WhiteHouse 'require' anything? The WhiteHouse is on trial, isn't it?"
David Spindoc: "I'm sorry, I couldn't hear you and that's all the time I have. Thanks."

The Partisan Phase of the Senate Trial, Part 1: Three Pitiful Witnesses

And so subpoenas were prepared and delivered to Monica Lewinsky, Vernon Jordan and Sidney Blumenthal. Monica, to testify for the 23rd time as to her knowledge of the President's perjury and obstruction of Justice with a particular emphasis on determining if the President had in any way encouraged her to give false testimony. Vernon Jordan, an Attorney and close personal friend of Billy Jeff Clinton's, to testify as to whether his role in finding Monica a job was directed at 'taking care' of her for filing a false affidavit in the Jones lawsuit: and whether he had a hand in advising Monica to destroy or hide evidence. Sidney Blumenthal, to testify about the stories that the President had told him accusing Monica of being a stalker; and that the President said he had not 'done' Monica.

Each day the witnesses would testify and that evening the videotaped depositions were made available to Senators in private viewing rooms. The Senators, who were not jurors and should not be confused with jurors because that would lead to erroneous conclusions about their responsibilities in the impeachment trial, cleverly avoided the appearance of a 'rush to judgement'. After two of the videotapes had been available for days, less than ten percent of Senators had signed in to view the tapes.

Monica Lewinsky

We finally got to see the First Slut speak. She was described as 'young', 'self-possessed' and 'intelligent'.

They forgot to mention, 'well-prepared' and 'still trying to cover up for the President'.

The questioning started with Monica relating her full name for the record. Monica Samille Lewinsky. Samille. Like, 'Samille, you're on candid camera'. As in, "I really liked her samille". Could having a middle name like that have had something to do with Monica's oral fixation? We'll just have to leave that question for the behaviorists out there. But it sure is interesting. (Let's all take a moment to pause and than God that her middle name wasn't Analle.)

And here we find ourselves talking about that girl's big mouth again. When asked with whom she had discussed her Presidential sexual relationship, Monica responded:

Q. Ms. Lewinsky, did you tell a number of people in varying details about your relationship with the President?
A. Yes.
Q. ..tell us who did you tell?
A. Catherine Allday Davis, Neysa Deman Erbland, Natalie Ungvari, Ashley Raines, Linda Tripp, Dr. Kathy Estep, Dr. Irene Kassorla, Andy Bleiler, my mom, my aunt. Who else has been subpoenaed?
Q. Okay. Let me suggest Dale—did you mention Dale Young?
A. Dale Young. I'm sorry.
     From Monica's Videotaped Deposition

We can all be appreciative that Monica never got a job in the NSA. I assume she asked who else had been subpoenaed so that she could tell them, too. If you examine this you would soon realize that virtually every living person on that planet knew about the President and

Monica, with the possible exception of you and me. She admits to telling at least eleven people that she has a sexual relationship with the President of the United States. How long, on average, do you think it took for each of those persons to tell their best friend? I'd guess about seven seconds. And then how long do you suppose it took for each one of *them* to tell *their* best friend? You get the picture.

Monica objected when the House Managers referred to the 'salacious' content of her earlier testimony. She wanted them to refer to them as her 'encounters' because, 'Hey, we're talking about my relationship here.'

A. Can—can we—can you call it something else?

Q. Okay.
A. I mean, this is—this is my relationship—
Q. What would you like to call it?
A. —so, I mean, is—
Q. This is the—or this was—
A. It was my first encounter with the President, so I don't really see it as my first salacious—that's not what this was.
           From Monica's Videotaped Deposition

We have definitely got some real Wizards of the English Language working here. We have Billy Jeff Clinton with his 'is' and 'alone'. We have Senator Harkin with his masterful evisceration of the word 'juror'. And now we have Monica Lewinski, who walked in and gave the President a Blowjob the first chance they got, defining it as a romantic 'encounter'. Maybe they made eye contact while she serviced him. Maybe that's what Monica found romantic about it. Who knows? I, for one, am going to

sign up for an Ebonics course. Maybe they actually have
words and ideas in that language are shared and generally
understood. It's worth a look because this English language
has definitely developed some serious problems. I did
pretty well in school but I sure don't get it anymore.

Let's take a look at another example of the problem:

```
Q. Let me ask you, though—I realize none of
us were there—but that statement, 'I was
never really alone with Monica; right?'—that
was not—he was alone with you on many
occasions, was he not?
A. I—I'm not trying to be difficult, but I
feel very uncomfortable making judgments on
what someone else's statement when they're
defining things however they want to define
it. So if you—if you ask me, Monica, were you
alone with the President, I will say yes, but
I'm not comfortable characterizing what
someone else says—
Q. Okay.
A.—passing judgment on it. I'm sorry.
        From Monica's videotaped deposition
```

The House Manager was clearly trying to get Monica to
conclude that the President lied to the Grand Jury when
he said he was not alone with her. That made Monica
uncomfortable because it called for a judgement on her
part, poor thing. I mean, how could she make a judgment
on what someone else is saying when they're defining
things however they want to define it? So she could only
say that when *she* was asked if they were ever alone then
she would say yes. But if the person she was alone *with*
said no, they weren't alone, well then it would be

judgmental for her to call that a lie because that would call for her to make a judgement as to that persons definition of 'alone', right? Her testimony clearly exonerated the President of the perjury charge. That much should be clear to you now, if you will pay no attention to the man behind the curtain.

Monica's testimony covered the Obstruction of Justice charge as well as well.

Q. Now, you have testified in the grand jury. I think your closing comments was that no one ever asked you to lie, but yet in that very conversation of December the 17th, 1997 when the President told you that you were on the witness list, he also suggested that you could sign an affidavit and use misleading cover stories. Isn't that correct?
A. Uh—well, I—I guess in my mind, I separate necessarily signing affidavit and using misleading cover stories. So, does—
Q. Well, those two—
A. Those three events occurred, but they don't—they weren't linked for me.
Q. But they were in the same conversation, were they not?
A. Yes, they were.
Q. Did you understand in the context of the conversation that you would deny the—the President and your relationship to the Jones lawyers?
A. Do you mean from what was said to me or—
Q. In the context of that—in the context of that conversation, December the 17th—
A. I—I don't—I didn't—
Q. Okay. Let me ask it. Did you understand in the context of the telephone conversation

with the President that early morning of
December the 17th—did you understand that you
would deny your relationship with the
President to the Jones lawyers through use of
these cover stories?

A. From what I learned in that—oh, through
those cover stories, I don't know, but from
what I learned in that conversation, I
thought to myself I knew I would deny the
relationship.

Q. And you would deny the relationship to the
Jones lawyers?

A. Yes, correct.

Q. Good.

A. If—if that's what it came to.

Q. And in fact you did deny the relationship
to the Jones lawyers in the affidavit that
you signed under penalty of perjury; is that
right?

A. I denied a sexual relationship.

Q. The President did not in that conversation
on December the 17th of 1997 or any other
conversation, for that matter, instruct you
to tell the truth; is that correct?

A. That's correct.

Q. And prior to being on the witness list,
you—you both spoke—

A. Well, I guess any conversation in relation
to the Paula Jones case. I can't say that any
conversation from
the—the entire relationship that he didn't
ever say, you know, 'Are you mad? Tell me the
truth.' So—

Q. And prior to being on the witness list,
you both spoke about denying this
relationship if asked?

A. Yes. That was discussed.

Q. He would say something to the effect that—
or you would say that—you—you would deny

anything if it ever came up, and he would nod
or say that's good, something to that effect;
is that right?
A. Yes, I believe I testified to that.
    From Monica's videotaped deposition

So the President spoke to Monica, in a conversation at
2:30 in the morning, and told her she was on the witness
list for the Jones case, told her she could file an affidavit
to avoid testifying, and talked about 'cover stories'
(commonly referred to as 'lies'). But they weren't 'linked'
for her. Glad she cleared that up. Otherwise it may have
appeared to some of us poor, misunderstanding citizens
that the President was trying to Obstruct Justice.

He had also told her in that conversation that "it broke
his heart" that she was on that witness list. Billie Jeff
Clinton was feeling her pain. The guy is just *so* sensitive
and caring. One of the little fawns he had ministered to
was going to have to testify in that nasty Jones lawsuit.
He never gave even a thought to himself; he only cared
about her, his little fawn. Poor, broken hearted little
Billie Jeff Clinton, forced again to tote that bale of only
caring for others, never himself. You really do have to
love that guy.

There was further testimony about the affidavit.

Q. Did—did the subject of the affidavit come
up with the President?
A. Yes, towards the end of the conversation.
Q. And how did—tell us how that occurred.
A. I believe I asked him if he wanted to see
a copy of it, and he said no.

Q. Well, I mean, how did you introduce that
into the subject—into the conversation?
A. I don't really remember.
Q. Did he ask you, well, how's the affidavit
coming or—
A. No, I don't think so.
Q. But you told him that you had one being
prepared, or something?
A. I think I said—I think I said, you know,
I'm going to sign an affidavit, or something
like that.
Q. Did he ask you what are you going to say?
A. No.
Q. And this is the time when he said
something about 15 other affidavits?
A. Correct.
Q. And tell us as best as you can recall
what—how that—how that part of the
conversation went.
A. I think that was the—sort of the other
half of his sentence as, No, you know, I
don't want to see it. I don't need to—or,
I've seen 15 others.
It was a little flippant.
Q. In his answer to this proceeding in the
Senate, he has indicated that he thought he
had—might have had a way that he could have
you—get you to file a—basically a true
affidavit, but yet still skirt these issues
enough that you wouldn't be called as a
witness.
Did he offer you any of these suggestions at
this time?
A. He didn't discuss the content of my
affidavit with me at all, ever.
Q. But, I mean, he didn't make an offer that,
you know, here's what you can do, or let me
send you over something that can maybe keep
you from committing perjury?

A. No. We never discussed perjury.
Q. On—well, how did that conversation end?
Did you talk about anything else?
A. I said goodbye very abruptly.
    From Monica's videotaped testimony

So it was clear that the President had no knowledge of the contents of the affidavit whatsoever. It might appear to some that he had plenty of opportunity to take a peek. After all, Monica had testified that the Presidents best friend, Vernon Jordan, had helped edit it. But Vernon testified that he never saw it and we could all see how trustworthy his testimony was (once credit card receipts jogged his memory, at least). When Monica asked Billie Jeff if he would like a copy of her affidavit the President said no, clear evidence that he was completely independent of any of Monica's wrongdoing.

While it was true that both the President's own testimony and Monica's testimony revealed that they discussed cover stories in numerous conversations in which the affidavit was discussed, it was clear that the contents of the affidavit were *never* discussed. The cover stories and the affidavit were *not* 'linked'. And thus, the misunderstanding was cleared up. Let's all pay no attention to the man behind the curtain.

So Monica signed the false affidavit and took a trip the next day. Our busy little First Slut was keeping a lot of balls in the air. (It goes without saying that Monica had the Presidential Pair firmly in her grasp at the time as well.)

Q. Did—Mr. Carter, I assume, made those changes, and
then you subsequently signed the affidavit?
A. We worked on it in his office, and then, yes, I signed the affidavit.
Q. Is this the same day—
A. Yes.
Q.—at this point?
A. This was the 7th?
Q. Yes.
A. Correct.
Q. Did—did you take the signed—or a copy of the signed affidavit, I should say—did you take a copy—did you keep a copy?
A. Yes, I did.
Q. Did you give it to anyone or give anyone else a copy?
A. No.
Q. Now, did you, the next day on the 8th, go to New York for some interviews for jobs?
A. It was—it—I either went later on the 7th or on the 8th, but around that time, yes.

> From Monica's videotaped testimony

Sign the affidavit; go to New York for job interviews. Sign the affidavit; go to New York for job interviews set up by the best friend of the President. Sign the affidavit that the President had no knowledge of the content of, that you testified had been edited by his best friend, and go to New York for job interviews set up by that best friend of the President. Sign the affidavit that for all the President knew may have revealed the whole sordid affair and went on to accuse him of having non-consensual sex with Buddy, the First Dog, and go to New York for job interviews set up by the Presidents best pal. Right. Let's all close our eyes and plug our ears because the man behind the curtain we are paying no attention to is jumping up and down and waving and yelling and being generally *very* hard to pay no attention to.

But Monica needed to clear up a few more non-salacious details of her earlier testimony. There remained the matter of the role in all this of Vernon Jordan, the Presidents best friend.

Q. Let me direct your attention to your meeting with Vernon Jordan on December the 31st of 1997. Was that to go back and talk about the job again?
A. Little bit, but the—the—for me, the point of that meeting was I had gotten to a point where Linda Tripp wasn't returning my phone calls, and so I felt that I needed to devise some way, that somehow—to kind of cushion the shock of what would happen if Linda Tripp testified all the facts about my relationship, since I had never disclosed that to the President. So that was sort of my intention in meeting with Mr. Jordan, was hoping that I could give a little information and that would get passed on.
Q. This was at a meeting for breakfast at the Park Hyatt Hotel?
A. Yes.
Q. Were just the two of you present?
A. Yes.
Q. Did you discuss other things, other than Linda Tripp and your job search?
A. I think we talked about what each of us were doing New Year's Eve.
Q. Specifically about some notes that you had at your
apartment?
A. Oh, yes. I'm sorry.

Um, well, I mean, that really was in relation
to discussing Linda Tripp. So—
Q. And the Jones lawyers, too. Was that
right?
A. Um, I—I don't know that I discussed the
Jones lawyers. If I've testified that I
discussed the Jones lawyers, then I did, but—
Q. Okay. Well, tell us about the notes.
A. Well, the—sort of the—I don't know what to
call it, but the story that I gave to Mr.
Jordan was that I was trying to sort of alert
to him that, gee, maybe Linda Tripp might be
saying these things about me having a
relationship with the President, and right
now, I'm explaining this to you. These aren't
the words that I used or how I said it to
him, and that, you know, maybe she had seen
drafts of notes, trying to obviously give an
excuse as to how Linda Tripp could possibly
know about my relationship with the President
without me having been the one to have told
her. So that's what I said to him.
Q. And what was his response?
A. I think it was something like go home and
make sure—oh, something about a—I think he
asked me if they were notes from the
President to me, and I said no. I know I've
testified to this. I stand by that testimony,
and I'm just recalling it, that I said no,
they were draft notes or notes that I sent to
the President, and then I believe he said
something like, well, go home and make sure
they're not there.
Q. And what did you do when you went home?
A. I went home and I searched through some of
my papers, and—and the drafts of notes I
found, I sort of—I got rid of some of the
notes that day.
Q. So you threw them away?

```
A. Mm-hmm.
THE REPORTER: Is that a 'yes'?
THE WITNESS: Yes. Sorry.
        From Monica's Videotaped Deposition
```

This could spell **trouble** for Vernon Jordan. It could mean that Vernon Jordan, best friend of B.J. Clinton and respected attorney, might have committed an act that would constitute Obstruction of Justice. How would he respond to this? It was clear and convincing testimony by Monica Lewinsky, consistent with her earlier testimony on the matter, that Vernon Jordan, formerly head of the National Urban League, had told her to destroy evidence that would have a bearing on a Federal Civil Rights Lawsuit.

We turn now to the videotaped testimony of Vernon Jordan, Presidential pal, and certainly not a guy to be screwed with by some piss-ant House Manager in the Senate Impeachment trial of President B.J. Clinton.

Vernon Jordan

Vernon Jordan was able to clear up a little sticking point. It seems he had testified earlier that he had not even *met* with Monica Lewinski on January 31, 1997. She had, of course, testified that it was at that meeting that Mr. Jordan had told her to destroy any notes she might have about her relationship with the President.

Of course anyone would be expected to forget about a breakfast meeting with a young woman on New Years Eve in which you discuss affidavits relating to the innocence or guilt of the President of the United States. Most of us have done that at one time or another. And Vernon Jordan is a respected attorney associated with the WhiteHouse. Not the sort of person we have come to expect to remember a meeting like that.

Luckily the House Managers had been able to obtain a copy of the credit card receipt showing that Jordan had paid for the breakfast. Refreshed his memory. He remembered the meeting as soon as the receipt was shown to him. Remembered it clearly enough to remember that, at the meeting he just remembered, he did **not** tell her to get rid of her notes regarding the President (to the best of his memory, we assume). (Pay no attention to the man behind the curtain)

His testimony was truly hilarious. You would have to stick a string of firecrackers up a ferret's ass to see equivalent squirming action. Only a pained member of the weasel family can out-squirm a Washington attorney getting caught giving 'contradictory' testimony to the United States Senate. Let's listen in:

A. "If you would refer to my testimony before
the grand jury when asked about a
breakfast with Ms. Lewinsky on December
31st, I testified that I did not have
breakfast with Ms. Lewinsky on December
31st because I did not remember having had
breakfast with Ms. Lewinsky on December
31st. It was not on my calendar. It was New
Year's Eve. I have breakfast at the Park
Hyatt Hotel three or four times a week if
I am in town, and so I really did not
remember, and I told that to the grand
jury. It is clear, based on the evidence
here, that I was at the Park Hyatt on
December 31st. So I do not deny, despite my
testimony before the grand jury, that on
December 31st, that I was there with Ms.
Lewinsky, but I did testify before the
grand jury that I did not remember having
a breakfast with her on that date, and
that was the truth."

From Vernon's videotaped deposition

To summarize, he did not remember the meeting until
the credit card receipt was presented to him. But he did
remember, CLEARLY, that at the meeting he did not
remember, that Monica and he did not discuss either
destroying evidence and did not mention the name of Linda
Tripp. That much was clear.

Vernon Jordan further testified that his job search
for Monica Lewinsky was conducted when he had time but
without any real pressure, and certainly *no* pressure from
the WhiteHouse. It must have been pure coincidence that
Vernon Jordan put out what appeared to be a huge effort
for Monica Lewinsky. Ronald Perelman testified that in Mr.
Jordan's 12 years on Revlon's board, he had only called

him once on behalf of a job candidate: a "terrific young girl", Monica Lewinsky. Mr. Jordan's call to Ron Perelman came within minutes of a five-minute conversation with Ms. Lewinsky, who called him from New York, coincidentally right about the time that she was filing her false affidavit in the Paula Jones case. After talking to Ron Perelman, Vernon Jordan called Monica Lewinsky right back to tell her that he had made the call. When she got the job the next day, she called him again and they spent seven minutes on the phone congratulating each other on their success. About an hour later he called her yet again and they had a three-minute conversation in which he says he urged her to accept and that $40,000 was good pay for the first real job she had ever had in her life. All this, of course, was Pure Coincidence; nothing had anything to do with anything else that was going on. (Pay no attention to the man behind the curtain)

Vernon Jordan also testified that he did not know of the President's affair until it was made public in January of 1998. He would have us believe that he, The Presidents Best Friend, his golfing buddy, the guy the President had dinner with on Christmas Eve every year, his attorney confidant and main fixer, had been blissfully unaware of the Presidents affair. (He sounded a lot like Colonel Klink from Hogan's Heroes. "I know nothing!") He clearly remembered that he knew nothing: when he remembered.

Miss Lewinsky says she told Vernon Jordan of her Oval Office sex sessions many weeks earlier, long before she filed her false affidavit in the Paula Jones sexual harassment case. She says Vernon Jordan helped draft the affidavit and colluded with her in deleting a reference to her being alone with B.J. Clinton. But that's not the way

Vernon Jordan remembered it. In fact, he remembered not remembering it that way with absolute clarity. (Pay no attention to the man behind the curtain)

Vernon Jordan testified he had forgotten virtually all of the content of many telephone calls to and from the White House in the weeks prior to the mushroom cloud of the Lewinsky scandal appearing on the horizon on Jan 21. But he was *positive* they had nothing to do with the young woman in the middle of it, a young woman he was trying to find a job for on the Presidents behalf. He forgot the content of all those phone calls, but he remembered that they were not about Lewinsky. Clearly.

Do you get the feeling that if it wasn't for irritating blue dresses and restaurant receipts this whole thing would have gone a bit differently?

'Mother wit' causes me to believe that Vernon Jordan thinks we and the House Managers and the Senate have no wit. 'Mother wit' causes me to believe that Vernon Jordan thinks we can't recognize a mother when we see one. Vernon Jordan would be most pleased, I believe, if we would just, *please*, pay no attention to the man behind the curtain.

Sidney Blumenthal

Sidney Blumenthal testified that his position was that of Assistant to the President and that dealing with the press was one of his primary responsibilities. Sidney Blumenthal testified again as to the conversations he had with the President. These were the pre-Blue-Dress conversations when the President planned on trashing Monica Lewinsky in the media by denying the whole thing and accusing her of being a stalker and a wacko loser. (A bit of the old pot calling the kettle black, in fact)

Shortly after the Lewinsky story broke there were a number of articles in the press, attributed to WhiteHouse sources, that referred to Monica as having weight problems, and that she was called 'The Stalker.' They went on to say that she was known as a flirt, wore her skirts too short, and was 'a little bit weird.'

It seemed a rather incredible coincidence that these stories sounded almost *exactly* like the stories that the President had told Sidney Blumenthal. But we should be getting used to incredible, but unrelated, coincidences by now. (Pay no attention to the man behind the curtain)

Then Blumenthal stepped into the crap. He was asked if he had any knowledge of how the stories that Clinton had told him had leaked out of the WhiteHouse. Remember that Sidney Blumenthal's role in the WhiteHouse appeared to some to have consisted *primarily* of leaking stories to the press. And, of course, denying it when asked.

Well, Mr. Blumenthal denied it under *oath* this time. Seems that House Managers were already aware that a pal of Blumenthal's had stated that Blumenthal had leaked the story to the press within days of his meeting with the

President. After Blumenthal testified the House Managers contacted Christopher Hitchens, Blumenthal's pal, and obtained an affidavit in which he swore that, "during lunch on March 19, 1998, in the presence of myself and Carol Blue, Mr. Blumenthal stated that Monica Lewinsky had been a 'stalker' and that the President was 'the victim' of a predatory and unstable sexually demanding young woman. I have knowledge that Mr. Blumenthal recounted to other people in the journalistic community the same story."

Yes, Mr. Blumenthal, you may have already won! A beautiful sealed indictment may already be yours! An all expense paid trip to a Federal Pen may be waiting for you. You'll enjoy several years rooming with Bubba the Jailhouse Bully in luxurious accommodations, complete with a stainless steel in-room bathroom. You'll have the opportunity to study Law and realize that your mistake was that you forgot to not remember. You will learn what those trained to work in a Lawyer's world know. "Never Lie: Forget, Don't recall, Don't Recollect, Don't Remember, but NEVER EVER LIE, Under Oath; Otherwise Go For It."

If Bubba gives you time to learn that lesson well you'll make a good attorney someday. You'll obviously have no trouble with the ethics part of the exam as you've got that part down already.

Have a nice trip and don't forget to write.

The Partisan Phase of the Senate Trial, Part 2: Closing Arguments

The House Managers, a.k.a. The Thirteen White Guys, presented their closing arguments to the Senate.

James Brogan:

Described Monica Lewinsky as a bright woman, whose life has been forever marked. (Like the Blue Dress) He outlined her educational background and the fact that she had obtained a Masters in Psychology and had worked 'helping clients work on social skills'. James Brogan did not speculate on the specific sorts of 'social skills' that Monica Lewinsky might have been able to assist them with, and tactfully did not liken it to a Giving Head Start program for 'twenty-somethings'.

He went on to discuss allegations that the President of the United States, in an effort to discredit her and protect himself, had chosen to call his favorite honey names. The President was not alleged to have called Monica Lewinsky a 'skank', a 'pig', a 'loony bitch' and a girl who would suck the chrome off the bumper hitches of the San Francisco Forty Niner's if she had half a chance. But the President had certainly called her something bad.

He described the gifts that the President had given to Monica Lewinsky, allegedly to get her to keep the affair quiet. The gifts included a hatpin, a 12-lb. tub of thong degreaser, a gift certificate for a dozen of 'them good crescent rolls from France', a subscription to 'TrailerPark Living' magazine, a tin of Bag Balm and a copy of the 'Gold' edition AOL membership cdrom.

He didn't close his remarks by calling on the President to 'go fuck himself', but you could tell he would have liked to.

Asa Munchkinson

Asa Munchkinson described in detail the Presidents convoluted efforts to tamper with witnesses and obstruct justice. He detailed the efforts of Vernon Jordan to find Monica Lewinsky a job. Asa made no allegation that Vernon Jordan had, in his extraordinary effort to get Monica hired, told Ronald Perlman that "The President says she's the best blowjob this side of AirForce One. She'll do you, she'll do your Executive Committee, she'll do your best friend if you ask her to." Asa didn't mention that he was the prosecuting attorney who helped B.J. Clinton's brother experience the joys of Guilty on a Felony drug bust. He refrained from calling the President 'white trash', but you could tell he would have liked to.

Rep. Charles Canada

Charles Canada spoke about the Senate Trial Procedures, including the Six Parts of the Bipartisan Phase of the Senate Trial and criticized the Procedures as being formulated to legitimize an outcome. He did not twice describe the Senate as 'you assholes', but you could tell he wanted to.

Rep. George Geekas

Rep. Geekas made an impassioned presentation, refraining from asking the Democrat Senators, in so many words, to stop 'pimping their nieces' to acquit President B.J. Clinton.

Rep. Bob Burr

Bobby, one of the most respected and well liked members of the House of Representatives, pointed out he had it on good authority that 'even some Negroes' thought B.J. Clinton was guilty.

Rep. Chris Dannon

Dannon outlined that the Presidents Defense was 'just like an economy sized box of Twinkies'. It looked pretty substantial but they were 'all gone before you even got home from the store'. He concluded his remarks by asking if they could take a break for 'snack time'.

Rep. Steve Buyit

Steve Buyit argued convincingly for a 'finding of fact'. He articulated his belief that the term High Crimes and Misdemeanors did most certainly include repeatedly asking an intern for a facial and then lying about it to a Grand Jury and trying to obstruct justice.

Rep. James Bunsenburner

Bunsenburner described the President's defense as an 'Emperor Has No Clothes' defense. He pointed out that while Clinton did, in fact, have clothes, his pants were down around his ankles and he was trying to do magic tricks to distract everyone's attention from the intern he was resting his elbows on.

Rep. Ed Hydrant

Ed spoke to the polls. He discussed the fact that the Democrats had been following the polls like hookers following their potential johns down the street. He pointed out that 80% of the people in America had concluded the President was guilty in spite of the pitiful three witnesses they had been allowed to see. That being the case, 'won't you all vote guilty?'

Rep. Lindseed Graham

Lindseed Graham was my personal favorite. Earlier in the trial, while discussing the President's 2:30 am phone call to Monica Lewinsky, he pointed out that in his home state when you got a phone call at two am the person calling was, by definition, up to no good. Lindseed asked rhetorically how you could be truthful and misleading at the same time, as the President apparently wanted us to believe. Vernon Jordan would be well advised to call Lindseed Graham if he would really like to find 'Mother Wit' because Lindseed Graham has got it.

Bill McGollum

Bill outlined the 'Jane Does' for the benefit of the Senators who were having trouble keeping them all straight.

Jane Doe #1: Kathleen Willey, grope victim

Jane Doe #2: Gennifer Flowers,

Jane Doe #3: Paula Jones, witness to Clinton's leftist leaning.

Jane Doe #4: Monica Lewinsky, the First Slut

Jane Doe #5: Juanita Broderick, rape victim

Jane Doe #6: Buddy, the Presidential Dog

Jane Doe #7: Brownie Troop #263

Unfortunately, due to time constraints, Mr. McGullom was not able to list out the other 628 Jane Does.

Rep. Henry Hide

Henry Hide spoke with his usual eloquence and understatement. He avoided poor word choices like "Piece of Shit" when referring to the President and focused his statement on the issues. His statement was so focused, accurate and eloquent that he provided no grist for this mill.

The Rebuttal

Having lost the coin toss, the President's attorneys were now allowed to present the Final Defense of the President. My recollection of it goes something like this:

Mr. Charles RuffnPuff

"Honorable Senators who are not jurors, but who are, nonetheless, not to be tampered with; you have heard the arguments of the House Mangers and have no doubt concluded, based upon the facts, that my client, William Jefferson Clinton, 'B.J.' to his friends, is guilty of the crimes of perjury and obstruction of justice. But I am here to tell you; their case is one of Moving Targets, and Empty Pots. Moving Targets, and Empty Pots. Now, I really don't know what I mean by that when I say Moving Targets, and Empty Pots. I was trying to figure out what to say to you today and it just came to me. Moving Targets, and Empty Pots. Just try to work with me on this.

The real issue is whether the crimes committed by my client, William Jefferson Clinton, 'B.J.' to his friends and campaign contributors, except the Chinese, who refer to him as 'Mista Plesiden'; Rise to the Level of Removable Offenses. While it is true that the phrase, 'Rise to the Level of Removable Offenses', is a new one, coined by necessity with the death of the 'Rise to the Level of Impeachable Offenses' Defense, it really does provide us with a basis to weasel out of this mess. Moving Targets, and Empty Pots.

Clearly the House Managers just want to win this case too much. They have worked late night after night researching and investigating and preparing. Clear signs of their aggressive White Maleness. Now it's true that I am White, but I am handicapped and we do have a Black person on this defense team and we look a lot more like America than Thirteen White Guys any day of the week. I'm sure you agree. Moving Targets, and Empty Pots.

Take a look at the Articles of Impeachment themselves, gentle and tactful Senators who are not jurors and should not be confused with jurors. The Articles of Impeachment are, on their face, deficient. They are almost incomprehensible. In fact, the word 'is' is contained in them in over 43 instances. They start out with the assertion that the President 'is' guilty. This, in a country that presumes innocence and accepts the plausible deniability of the definition of 'is'? Moving Targets, and Empty Pots.

The Prosecution's case lacks *balance*, kind Senators of whom many are dependent upon the accused for campaign financing but are nonetheless unbiased. Sure the Prosecution presented lots of examples of lying and obstructing justice by the President of the United States. But did they once point out the several times he told the truth? Seems a little unfair and biased to omit that, don't you think? It lacks *balance* and *fairness*. Let me give you an example.

In his Grand Jury testimony William Jefferson Clinton, 'B.J.' to his friends, stated when asked, "When was the last time you spoke to Monica Lewinsky?" and I quote from the transcript now:

> "I'm trying to remember. Probably sometime before Christmas, or Kwanzaa. She came by to see Betty

sometime before Christmas, or Kwanzaa; or maybe
it was Ramadan. And she was there talking to her,
and I stuck my head out, said hello to her."

So you see, kind Senators who are not jurors as correctly
pointed out by the esteemed legal scholar Tom Harkin, the
President told the truth. He said, right in front of the
Grand Jury, that she was there and he "*stuck his head
out*"! If you've read the Starr report you know exactly
what he was referring to. I won't go into it here for fear
of upsetting the tactful decorum of these collegial
chambers. But clearly, the President told the truth when
he said he '*stuck his head out*'. Those Thirteen White
Guys didn't point that out to you did they? No. They
didn't. Moving Targets, and Empty Pots.

I could rest my case right here but I won't. Not
because I need to go on, but because stopping now would
completely screw up the networks and that would upset
the fabulous economy we all now enjoy. By the way have
you seen the latest price on Amazon.com? Freakin
Unbelievable, isn't it? Talk about yer Moving Targets and
yer Empty Pots! But I digress.

The Prosecutors of The Apostle of Progress and Hope,
'B.J.' to his friends, based a lot of their case on the
assumption that giving my client a one time pass on High
Crimes and Misdemeanors would threaten the Nation and
the Rule of Law. That it would somehow set back Civil
Rights in this nation because it is rooted in the Federal
Civil Rights lawsuit filed by Paula Jones. While it is true
that Paula Jones is a woman, let me ask you this; is she
handicapped or Black? No, gentle Senators, she is just

white. She doesn't *look* like America anymore that those Thirteen White Guys do. To presume she looks like America is to assume that the majority of Americans have big noses and morals. Clearly not the case. My associate, Ms. Cheryl Mills, who is also a woman, has assured you that Civil Rights are safe in this President's hands. Who are you Senators who are not jurors going to believe on Civil Rights, Thirteen White Guys or a Black Woman? I don't think we need to discuss *that* issue anymore. Moving Targets, and Empty Pots.

Let's turn now to that bothersome oath you took at the beginning of this trial. You swore to render impartial justice, didn't you? But did you hear Senator Byrd's comments on the television? Senator Byrd is widely regarded as the Sage of the Constitution and very well respected. He doesn't speak often but when he does you guys listen, right? I mean, if Senator Byrd farts you can bet that ninety-nine of you will bend over and take a whiff. I'm not wrong on this, am I? You bet I'm not.

Well, Senator Byrd stated on National Television that he had concluded that President B.J. Clinton **was** guilty of the crimes he is accused of. He came up with the same answer you did on that one. He said he had concluded that the crimes **do** rise to the level of Impeachable and Removable Offenses. He came up with the right answer on that one too.

But Senator Byrd went on to say that he was going to vote to acquit the President anyway because the President is popular. We just wish he'd said that a couple of weeks ago.

Moving Targets and Empty Pots? Screw it. This case is over and Senator Byrd has shown all of us the path out of the wilderness. You are all Senators and your only responsibility is to get re-elected. Live the moment, gentlemen. Screw the case. Screw the Rule of Law. Screw the Constitution. Screw your Oath.

I rest my case."

The Partisan Phase of the Senate Trial, Part 3: The Final Secret Senate Meeting

And so it was time for the Senate to Secretly Deliberate. Names are omitted from the following transcript of the Final Secret Senate Meeting to preserve the Secrecy of the meeting and preserve the collegial decorum of the Senate.

Senator of the Evil Empire: "We'll call the Secret Meeting to order. Sergeant at Arms, have the doors been sealed and has the room been cleared?"
Sergeant at Arms: "Yes, the room is secure, Sir."
Senator of the Evil Empire: "Ok, here's where we stand. The President's poll numbers have continued to hold up in spite of the obvious fact of his guilt. I know that I, for one, sure don't understand it. I swear that if the President were found to be the ringleader behind the curtain of secrecy surrounding the child porn industry then the bastard's popularity would jump ten points. But there we have it."
Caring Senator: "Quit your bitching and let's get on with this, Trent. This trial is over and you know it. It was over a couple of weeks ago when we voted unanimously, if you ignore the votes of the Republicans and a Democrat, in favor of Senator Byrd's motion to dismiss the trial."
Senator of the Evil Empire: "I know that's your position, Tom, but I still fail to understand how any of us can vote to acquit in face of the obvious fact of the President's guilt. Remember, we took an oath to do impartial justice."
Caring Senator: "Oath Shmoath, we're Senators and responsible to no-one. Nobody gets to review our decision

or appeal our decision. What we say goes on this matter. Let's vote and get it over with. We need to get back to the work of the American people and that means getting back to getting re-elected."

Senator of the Evil Empire: "We have to debate, the rules say we have to debate."

Caring Senator: "Yea, I guess you're right. We would be shirking our duty if we violated our oath to do impartial justice without debating it first. Fine."

Senator of the Evil Empire: "Thanks, Tom, that's very bipartisan of you. Who wants to go first?"

Caring Senator 2: "Me, Me, Me, Me, Me. C'mon you guys, let me go first."

Senator of the Evil Empire: "Go ahead, Paul, do your Mr. Potato-head thing for us."

Caring Senator 2: "Just what the hell do you mean by that, Trent?"

Senator of the Evil Empire: "You look like Mr. Potato-Head, Wellstone. Your facial features are so jumbled up you look like the 'before' in an advertisement for gene therapy."

Caring Senator 2: "Fine, well I guess tact and decorum went out the door with the television cameras."

Senator of the Evil Empire: "Good to see you are finally starting to figure things out, Mr. Potato-head. Now speak your piece or your time is up."

Caring Senator 2: "No problem, butt-wad. I'd just like to say that since we are not jurors we can vote any way we want. As my colleague, Tom Barkin, correctly pointed out; since we don't get box lunches or jury pay we have no responsibility to abide by any normal juror rules."

Senator of the Evil Empire: "Thanks for your contribution to justice, Mr. Tom Barkin's Lap Dog. Run along, now, your master is blowing your dog whistle. Next."

Caring Senator 3: "I resent your calling Paul my lapdog."

Senator of the Evil Empire: "So what. Do you have anything to contribute to this debate or not? And I don't think any of us care to hear any more of your stupid diatribes on the definition of 'juror', you moron."

Caring Senator 3: "I am NOT a moron, jerk. I just fail to understand how you and most of the Republicans can conclude from the evidence that the President is guilty of High Crimes and Misdemeanors."

Senator of the Evil Empire: "Tom, I can explain it to you but, unfortunately, I cannot understand it for you. Your insipid smile is adequate evidence of your intellectual capacity. Do you have anything more to add?"

Caring Senator 3: "Yes, I feel that I must state for the record that I am not a moron and I am not a juror. I think future historians will agree with me on that."

Senator of the Evil Empire: "You are definitely not a juror, Tom. Next."

Senator from Scotland: "Trent, I'd like to discuss the issue I raised for the cameras the other day. I feel we're all in a real pickle here. You know, trapped between our oath to do impartial justice and our need to follow the polls and acquit the President in spite of the overwhelming evidence. If we all vote 'not proven', like the Scottish do, we can squirm out of this one while preserving reasonable doubt that we actually did our duty. What do you think?"

Senator of the Evil Empire: "Great idea, Scotty! Afterwards we can all go out and throw some poles on the rotunda. Brilliant. Next."

Senator of the Evil Empire 2: "I would like to speak to the people here from both parties who are contemplating voting to acquit the President. You are doing so because you have decided to follow the polls that show that the American people don't want the President removed from office. I would just like to ask you all to consider how the voters are going to feel about it when the next 'bimbo eruption' or scandal hits. Billie Jeff Clinton does not seem to be capable of learning from his mistakes and the American people just don't trust him anymore. The next thing you know we're going to find out that the bastard committed a rape or was found in a men's room with PeeWee Herman or something. You should consider that before you cast a vote to acquit."

Senator of the Evil Empire: "Good point, Gordy."

Caring Senator: "That's ridiculous, I half expect you to next imply that the President handed nukes to a foreign government or something. Nice Try."

Senator of the Evil Empire: "I wouldn't put it past him. Next."

Moderate Republican Senator: "Trent, I can't go back to Maine and get re-elected if I vote to impeach the President. I'm just not convinced that voters would respect me in the morning if I stood on principle and voted to impeach."

Senator of the Evil Empire: "No problem, sweetheart, you just vote however you want. Just don't be looking to the Republican Party for a whole lot of funding when you get back to Maine if you vote to acquit. The Republican Party doesn't support people who are completely stupid or unethical. Next."

Caring Senator 4: "Trent, do you have to be so unreasonable here? You need to get some help with your self-esteem or visit a psychic vortex or something. You're getting all wrapped up in this. You clearly want to win too much. It's just not gonna happen so let's just get on with the vote. I mean, can't we all just get along?"

Senator of the Evil Empire: "Well Gebby, you're right about getting on to the voting. To hell with this stupid and pointless debate. Mr. Chief Justice, would you have a problem if we just called for quiet time so we can all take naps and get ready for the rush to the cameras tonight?

Senator of the Evil Empire: "Mr. Chief Justice?"

Senator of the Evil Empire: "Mr. Chief Justice?"

Caring Senator: "He's asleep, Trent. I think he exhausted himself laughing at us."

Senator of the Evil Empire: "Thanks Tom. Well I'll take that as his agreement with my motion. So it's Naptime boys and girls. Sergeant at Arms, see to it that you wake us up with time to fix the bad hair before the doors open."

Sergeant at Arms: "No problem, Trent, have a nice nap."

The Partisan Phase of the Senate Trial
Part 3.1: The Vote

On February 12, 1999 the Senate of the United States voted to acquit Billie Jeff Clinton on both of the counts against him.

The votes came out with 45 Senators voting guilty on the perjury charge and 50 Senators voting guilty on the obstruction of justice charge, all Republicans. As there were 55 Republican Senators you can easily do the math and determine that ten Republicans voted to acquit on the perjury charge and 5 voted to acquit on the obstruction of justice charge. Every Democrat voted to acquit on both charges. (Pay no attention to the man behind the curtain of the Democrat Fund Raising Machine.)

Billie Jeff Clinton had promised not to hold another pep rally on the WhiteHouse lawn after the vote. He promised not to hold any big parties after the vote. He promised not to play the bongo drums and smoke big stogies after the vote. And, as near as we can tell, Billie Jeff Clinton kept his promise. The President was not reported to have had phone sex with anyone that evening. Instead, Billie Jeff Clinton apparently spent a quiet evening at home with the little woman. One could well imagine that it was very quiet, and very, very cold. But that assumes that the First Lady really gives a damn about anything but the power.

Aftermath and Legacy

By 73 percent to 18 percent, voters concluded that
Clinton perjured himself before the Grand Jury; by 53 to
35, they think that he obstructed justice. By 73 percent
to 15 percent, they understand that the Democratic
Senators who voted to acquit President Clinton did so
because they supported their party, not because they
believed Clinton was innocent.

Now, I'm no great believer in polls but I can tell you
that these polls sure seemed to square with my own
conclusions for a change. From my perspective they
seemed to pass the 'reasonable man' test a lot more clearly
than the polls we had been seeing earlier.

After the acquittal B.J. Clinton held a press
conference where he almost apologized again. "Well, of
course, I've learned a lot of personal lessons, most of
which I have already discussed-and presidents are people,
too," he said. He said he had an "enormous amount of
respect" for the U.S. Constitution, the framers of it, and
the American People. "And my advice to future presidents
would be to decide what you believe you ought to do for
the country and focus on it and work hard. The American
people hire you to do that and will respond if you work at
it and if they sense that you're doing this for them," he
said.

Billie Jeff Clinton was explaining for Future Presidents
that his Presidency, which would be remembered for his
hard work on such accomplishments as HealthCare Reform,
The Largest Tax Hike in U.S. History, Waco, Wag the Dog,
and Monica and Paula, proved that the American people will

respond if you work hard. Hope everyone was taking notes on that little gem. We all know that future Presidents will be looking to Billie Jeff as a fine example of Leadership and self-sacrifice for the American people.

Two days after the acquittal vote, on Valentines Day, February 14, 1999 the following poem was printed in a Washington newspaper:

> **STUPID**
> Sorry I took,
> So long to respond.
> You did a great job,
> On my left-leaning wand.
> I'm sorry I told,
> Some little white lies.
> Would you do me again?
> (Between other guys)
> **HANDSOME**

Over the following weeks Hillary started making noise about running for the Senate seat in New York. The press got real excited about that but were silent as to whether she would run as the wife of the soon to be former Impeached President or as the former wife of the soon to be former Impeached President. For a few days it seemed that the Hillary for Senate story was going to dominate the press for months to come. Could anything be more interesting or important?

Then Juanita Broderick came forward. Broderick alleged, very convincingly, that a younger and stronger Billie Jeff Clinton had raped her some 21 years ago. It was Clearly Not an Impeachable Offense. The Statute of Limitations made it moot and the Founding Fathers said nothing about 21 year old convincing charges of rape. The Framers of the Constitution would have written clear language in the Constitution had they ever wanted a President removed for perjury, obstruction of justice or old rape cases. Move along, people, there's nothing to see here. Go back to your homes.

Next came Monica Lewinsky's book. It could have been titled "Blown Cover", "It worked out to $250,000 per Blowjob" or "7 Insipid Habits of Successful Home Wrecking Sluts" or something like that. In it, Monica described how 'terrorized' she felt when Starr's prosecutors cornered her in a hotel room. "It felt like someone had slit open my belly and poured acid inside", she said. So sad it is that such action is not within the powers of the Special Prosecutors office. Ken Starr could have earned back $40 million worth of goodwill in one fell swoop.

It seems that Ken Starr's prosecutors told Monica in that room that she could be prosecuted for her earlier lies under oath in the Paula Jones case. She asked to call her attorney and the prosecutors told Monica that if she did that the deal was off. She asked to call her mother and they ridiculed her. The Bastards! This distressed Monica to no end. Obviously Monica was not adequately familiar with her Miranda Rights:
"You have the right to remain silent. You have the right to an attorney. You have the right to call your mommy. But do any one of these things and the deal is off and you just might just spend the next 27 years giving blow jobs to prison guards, you skanky slut."

(Or something to that effect.)

All this distressed Monica to the point of contemplating suicide. She gave serious consideration to throwing herself out the window of the tenth floor hotel room they were in. Monica, simple, sweet girl that she is, failed to understand that you need serious power tools to open a tenth floor window of any hotel. And that, had she gotten the window open, it would have taken a ten pound tub of bag balm and a healthy shove by several of the prosecutors to get her through the window. And, had she gotten out the window, that given her surface area it would be extremely doubtful that she could reach a killing terminal velocity in only ten floors. But she's young, and a psychology major, and not to be expected to understand such complexities.

Monica further explained in her book that her 'affair' with the President did not interfere with official business because they were 'together mostly on the weekends'. I'm sure we are all relieved to know that the empty headed skank has reassured us on this point. Puts the Year of National Bullshit that B.J. and Monica put us all through into perspective, doesn't it?

Monica told in her book of her affair with, and becoming pregnant by, a Pentagon official (single guy, amazingly enough) and having an abortion, all this occurring during the time she was involved in her sweetly romantic affair with Billie Jeff. (My guess would be that Billie Jeff was not terribly troubled to hear this.) In a hypothetical interview Monica might have explained her reasons for disclosing this:

Interviewer: "Monica, why did you tell in your book about getting pregnant by a Pentagon official and having an abortion during the time you were involved with the President."

Monica: "I felt that I had to tell about that because I didn't want anyone to ever think that I had become pregnant by the President."

Interviewer: "So you were concerned that some might assume that the baby you had sucked into a sink was Billie Jeff's child?"

Monica: "Yes, some might had said that, even though I simply could not have become pregnant by the President."

Interviewer: "Because you two only had oral sex?"

Monica: "Yes, and I was taking an oral contraceptive at the time, so it was not possible."

Interviewer: "Excuse me?"

Monica: "We were having oral sex but I was taking oral contraceptives, so I could not have become pregnant with the President's baby."

Interviewer (muttering): "jesus"

Monica next did an interview with Barbara Walters. Two full hours filled with Monica's vacuous prattle and over 70 million Americans watched it. Truth be told, many viewers wanted to give Monica a shot at redeeming herself from widespread assumptions that she was simply an empty headed pig. Subsequent polls indicated that viewers believed, by six to one, that their previous assumptions were much too harsh on pigs.

Next came the Andrew Morton interviews. Andrew Morton is the author of the unforgettable biography of Princess Di. That autobiography is unforgettable primarily because of all the unsold copies we all see staring at us from discounted bookracks in grocery stores and booksellers throughout the world. Andrew revealed in interviews that, after spending time with Monica and learning the intimate details of her relationship with B.J. Clinton (and several other, primarily married, men) he understood the character of both Monica and Billie Jeff and, "knew which one he would prefer to spend a night in a foxhole with". I'd have to agree. She doesn't bomb foreign countries or seem to lie quite as much. And she *does* have a nice smile. If ya catch my drift.

Next out was George Stephanopoulos with his book about his time working for Clinton. If you consider 'withering stares' and "tense meetings" to be high drama or action you will love George Stephanopoulos' book. George dramatically told the unforgettable story of the devastation of getting 'hives' because he was under such incredible stress. Imagine the Horror.

George's tale takes us through his initial infatuation with the President. Apparently George was like a puppy with a new owner for Bill. Just LOVED that man. (In a non sexual way, of course. Not that there would be anything wrong with that. Not if it were consensual. Certainly not impeachable.) George sat back like a hayseed fresh off the turnip truck and believed each of Bill's lies, no matter how implausible, until each was *proven* to be a lie. One after the other, in succession, little George swallowed each lie, never apparently having the capacity to recognize the aftertaste from the previous one. Every car salesman in the country wants to see George Stephanopoulos walk in to *his* dealership.

After about the six thousandth time George defended B.J. publicly based upon a lie B.J. had told him and then got clobbered because the Truth came out, George decided to leave Bill's employ. George is not, obviously, a particularly fast learner. Clinton's present staffers called Stephanopoulos 'disloyal' because of the book. Clinton's present staffers must, therefore, be 'loyal' and either completely brain dead or 'un-ethics-impaired' or they'd be resigning and writing books too.

Then the China scandals re-burst into the fore. You remember the Buddhist temples, right? Well, apparently, the Chinese stole the plans for some of our nice little high tech W-88 nukes from the Los Alamos laboratory and in 1996 the Administration found out about it. And did nothing about it. In fact, they pushed for Most Favored Nation Status for China, primarily because of their great track record on human rights, we guessed. Not doing anything about the espionage and pushing for Most Favored Nation status was completely unrelated to the Campaign contributions accepted by Bill Clinton and Al Gore. Really. Completely unrelated. (Please to pay no attention to the man behind the curtain.)

After the China espionage scandal broke the Administration noted with some fanfare that they had seen to it that the spy who had worked as Los Alamos unmolested with their knowledge for three years was going to be fired. Seems he refused to cooperate when asked about it. In the midst of the Administration's statements that they had been "actively investigating" the espionage for three years they finally got around to asking the spy about it. Hope they didn't threaten to censure him.

On the front page of my local newspaper two headlines were printed side by side. The first was about the Nuclear Spy charges related to China. The second was a story about how the U.S. was planning to pay Iraqi insiders to end the regime of Saddam Hussein. So our government kept the fact that the Chinese had stolen our specifications for compact and powerful Nuclear weapons a secret for three years; but was making a public announcement about plans to destabilize a foreign government by giving money to dissidents inside that country. Brilliant.

And the Census kicked off. Today I answered my door (did I mention I got one of the 100,000 housing vouchers Clinton promised?) to be greeted by a very nice older lady working on the census. She asked me if my address was my address. I said, "Excuse me?" She confirmed that she was asking if the number *on* my house was really the number *of* my house. I confirmed this important piece of intelligence data for her. Then she asked me if my street name was the actual name of my street. She made it clear that it was important to our government for me to confirm that the name *on* my street was the name *of* my street. I confirmed that as well. She thanked me and started to move on to the next home. I stopped her and asked if she was really walking down my clearly marked street walking up to the clearly marked homes to confirm that the numbers and street names could be confirmed by the residents. She indicated that, yes, that important task was, indeed, hers. It's good to see that government still works.

And so the Impeachment saga of B.J. Clinton and the TrailerPark Presidency ends. Our Impeached President remained in office. And our Government was back to work.

Y2K and Beyond the Millenium

During research for this book I was fortunate to encounter a modern day Oracle. The ranks of the Homeless in this country have swelled with the consolidation of the Psychic Network industry. Thousands have been laid off as company after company has been bought up in an effort to consolidate market share in that intensely competitive industry. As a result of that consolidation some of the finest professional psychics of our time are now enjoying the travel and outdoor life offered by Homelessness. During a long night under the I-15 underpass with four bottles of Thunderbird wine, one of these Oracles, Sista Bulubuwaji Wambuti-Hershfield revealed the following prophecies:

January 1, 2000
Thousands of Panic Stricken Americans Barricaded in Homes

Reports from all over the country have flooded in of Americans Barricaded in their homes in fear of the consequences of the Y2K Bug. While it has been consistently confirmed that there has been no discernable effect on anything, anywhere, due to the Y2K bug, with the exception of people barricading themselves in their homes, officials are concerned that people are barricading themselves in their homes. Percy Jackboot, head of the Federal Emergency Management Authority, put it this way from his barricaded home; "People need to come out of their homes. Our resources are stretched much too thin to effectively surround so many homes. It would take us weeks to bombard them all with loud music and tear gas and knock down all their walls and burn them and their children out like we did in Waco. To say nothing of the clerical overhead of coming up with excuses like the one about child abuse that we had to dream up for Waco. These people need to un-barricade themselves and get back to work. When they come out, we'll come out."

November, 2000
President Re-Elected
William Jefferson Clinton to Start Third Term
William Jefferson ('B.J.') Clinton was elected to his third term as President of the United States today. Since his public opinion poll numbers skyrocketed with the shocking revelation that 'B.J.' was the man behind the curtain of secrecy surrounding the child pornography industry in the United States, Clinton had been almost certain to take the election. When asked about the apparent constitutional question surrounding his re-election, B.J. stated, "I'm certain the Supreme Court will find a way to resolve this issue. Clearly the framers of the Constitution did not intend the word 'two' to be taken literally."

In a related story:
Hillary tosses in the Towel
Hillary Clinton, immediately after the President's victory speech, said that she would, "definitely not continue running for Senator in the State of New York' but would instead continue to serve as co-President. Unnamed

WhiteHouse sources revealed that the First Lady had
been concerned for some time that the State of New York
had not been warm to her New York State Health Care
Proposal, which called for the purchase of a Boeing 747
aircraft with a hairdresser and fighter escort.

Sometime in 1999
Monica, Bag Balm Split

The Bag Balm Corporation announced from their Midwest
headquarters that they would not renew Monica Lewinsky's
contract as company spokesperson. Jim Balm, Vice
President of Marketing, offered a tersely worded press
release, which indicated that
Monica Lewinsky's 'other obligations' precluded
consideration of renewal and were 'inconsistent' with the
company's image as a 'provider of quality Bag Balm'.
Sources inside the company indicate that company
officials were disturbed with Ms. Lewinsky's 'Got Milk'
advertisements for the American Milk Board.

Sometime in the Year 2001
Congress Passes Homonym Act

The Senate today voted approval for the Offensive
Homonym's of Yesteryear Elimination Act (OHYEA), and
the President is expected to sign it into law immediately
upon his return from Thailand, where he is said to be
negotiating a treaty eliminating trade barriers to the
importation of Thai prostitutes to the U.S. The OHYEA
bill makes illegal any homonym which is a homonym of any
word considered offensive by any U.S. Citizen who is Gay,
Handicapped, Black, Hispanic, arguably Female, or Fat.

Congressman Barney Fife, (D. Scotland) the bills sponsor, stated from his barricaded home, "Who among us could forget hearing a couple of years ago that the word Niggardly had been used for the first time in over 40 years in this country. With the passage of this bill we can rest assured that the word that sounds like the 'N' word will never again be used in this country, along with a whole bunch of other words which sound like the 'N' word, or other words equally offensive. No longer will sticks and stones break bones. For with passage of this bill, criminals will no longer have access to words that sound like words that could offend."

Sometime in the Year 2000
Oregon Health Care Organization Under Fire

Oregon Assisted Suicide Inc., the two-year-old Oregon firm specializing in assisted suicide, came under fire today from Right to Keep Living organizations for their "Life Sucks" advertising campaign. The commercials, which feature well known spokes-failures from the sports and entertainment industries, faced blistering criticism after a 16 year old Oregonian used her fathers credit card to pay for suicide assistance late last week. Company President Val Vladamir insisted his company had acted within the law and that; "teenagers have a right to be protected from invasions of their rights to privacy and free will. The girl's life sucked, she had applied for an internship and had we not intervened she could have ended up in the WhiteHouse someday."

In related news the company's stock reached record highs on reports that it's forth quarter earnings would exceed analysts expectations due to an extraordinary gain related to its' "Show Them You Care" program, which allows persons to purchase subscriptions which pay for the assisted suicide of another. This, in spite of news that the Justice Department is investigating the company for allegedly selling thousands of duplicate subscriptions in the names of B.J. Clinton, Al Gore and Monica Lewinsky.

Sometime in the year 2000
Falwell Site Wins Top Net Honors

Jerry Falwell's "GayWatch" web site won the Annual Site of the Year Award in the Humor That Thinks It's Being Taken Seriously category. Sporting over a half a million 'hits' a month since it's erection in 1999, the "GayWatch" site, sponsored by Falwell's National Organization Going Against Gays, (NOGAG), has 'outed' Tinky Winky, Barney the Dinosaur, and Mr. Rogers. Asked how he selects candidates for 'outing', Falwell stated that, "I just out the ones I would hit on if I was gay".

Appendix A:

Presidential Lies

"He who permits himself to tell a lie once, finds it much easier to do a second and third time, till at length it becomes habitual; he tells lies without attending to it, and truths without the world's believing him. This falsehood of the tongue
leads to that of the heart, and in time depraves all its good dispositions."
                     Thomas Jefferson

     Compiling a complete list of the lies of the Impeached President, Billie Jeff Clinton, would earn one a place in history equivalent to the builders of the pyramids. People of several thousand years from now would look at the list and think that mere humans could not have accomplished it. Cults would be formed who believed ancient astronauts must have come down to help. To avoid complete deforestation, printed lists of Clinton lies are reduced to representative samples.

Lies of Clinton as the Moral Leader

"No question that an admission of making false statements to government officials... is an impeachable offense." -- Bill Clinton, Arkansas Gazette, August 8, 1974, page 7-A

"The President should resign. He has lied to the American people, time and time again, and betrayed their trust..." -- Bill Clinton, re: Richard M. Nixon, 1974.

*"The other thing we have to do is to take
seriously the role in this problem of . . .
older men who prey on underage women. . . .
There are consequences to decisions and . . .
one way or the other, people always wind up
being held accountable."*
   --Bill Clinton, June 13, 1996, in a speech
   endorsing a national effort against teen
   pregnancy   [USNews: 9/21/98]

*"Undeniably, character does count for our
citizens, our communities, and our Nation,
and this week we celebrate the importance of
character in our individual lives... core
ethical values of trustworthiness, fairness,
responsibility, caring, respect, and
citizenship form the foundation of our
democracy, our economy, and our society...
Instilling sound character in our children is
essential to maintaining the strength of our
Nation into the 21st century."*
   --Federal Register, Presidential Document
   [#7043]

Lies of Clinton on the Campaign Trail

*"When I was in England I experimented with
marijuana a time or two, and I didn't like
it. I didn't inhale."*
   --Candidate Bill Clinton (The New York
   Times, 3/30/92)

*"The road to tyranny, we must never forget,
begins with the destruction of the truth."*
     Bill Clinton, Oct. 15, 1995 at the
     University of Connecticut.

" Every time Bush talks about trust it makes chills run up and down my spine. The way he has trampled on the truth is a travesty of the American political system."
- Presidential candidate Bill Clinton, describing his opponent (Federal News Service, 10/28/92)

"There's just no such thing as truth when it comes to him. He just says whatever sounds good and worries about it after the election."
Presidential candidate Bill Clinton describing his opponent, George Bush (Quoted in the American Spectator, 10/28/92)

"They've been exposed as the trash they are"
Bill Clinton, January 27, 1992, speaking about the allegations that he had a 12 year affair with Gennifer Flowers. *Arkansas Gazette*

Lies of the Intermediate Periods of Presidential Lies

Jan 21, 1998
"The relationship was not sexual, I know what you mean, and the answer is no."

"I did not ask anyone to tell anything other than the truth. There is no improper relationship"

"I'm going to do my best to cooperate with the investigation. ... I don't know what the facts are."

Jan 22, 1998
"I'd like for you to have more rather than less, sooner rather than later."

Jan 26, 1998
"That allegation is false. . . I have absolutely leveled with the American people."

"I did not have sexual relations with that woman"

Feb 5, 1998
"I've already said that the charges are false. ... and I think it's important that I go back and do the work."

Feb 6, 1998
"I told the truth in my deposition [about Gennifer Flowers], and I also did in 1992 ... on 60 Minutes."

Clinton True Classic Lies

"[I]t depends on how you define "alone" ... there were a lot of times when we were alone, but I never really thought we were."

"It depends on what the meaning of the word 'is' is"
- excerpts from Bill Clinton's grand jury testimony

Clintonian Evasions (I'm not lying, I'm evading. Pay no attention to the man behind the curtain)

Here is what Clinton had to say to the Grand Jury in his "complete and truthful" testimony, distilled down to its essence:

"I don't remember.. I don't know.. I'm not sure.. I have no idea.. I don't believe so.. I don't recall.. I don't think so.. I don't have any specific recollection.. I have no recollection.. Not to my knowledge: I just don't remember: I don't believe.. I have no specific recollection.. I might have.. I don't have any recollection of that.. I don't have a specific memory: I don't have any memory of that.. I just can't say.. I have no direct knowledge of that.. I don't have any idea.. Not that I recall.. I don't believe I did.. I can't remember.. I can't say.. I do not remember doing so.. Not that I remember.. I'm not aware.. I honestly don't know.. I don't believe that I did.. I'm fairly sure.. I have no other recollection.. I'm not positive.. I certainly don't think so.. I don't really remember.. I would have no way of remembering that.. That's what I believe happened.. To my knowledge, no.. To the best of my knowledge.. To the best of my memory.. I honestly don't recall.. I honestly don't remember.. That's all I know: I don't have an independent recollection of that.. I don't actually have an independent memory of that.. As far as I know: I don't believe I ever did that.. That's all I know about that.. I'm just not sure.. Nothing that I remember.. I simply don't know.. I would have no idea: I don't know anything about that.. I don't have

any direct knowledge of that.. I just don't
know.. I really don't know: I can't deny
that, I just ... I have no memory of that at
all."

       Excerpts from The Testimony of William
       Jefferson Clinton

     It's worth noting that the first "I don't remember"
was repeated 70 times during his testimony and the "I
don't know" was repeated over 60 times. Thomas
Jefferson's statement that "He who permits himself to
tell a lie once, finds it much easier to do a second and
third time, till at length it becomes habitual" certainly
nails young Billie Jeff Clinton right on his thick head.

Appendix B:

The Race Card

No event in America today could be complete without the playing of the Race Card, and the Impeachment and Trial of Billie Jeff Clinton was no exception. For Billie Jeff Clinton, in addition to being the Apostle of Progress and Hope, was America's first Black President.

It may have appeared to the uneducated among us that the issues surrounding the Presidents impeachment would necessitate that he be attacked, or at least abandoned, by the Black special interest groups and Black Spokespersons. People taking this erroneous view would do so based upon the assumption that champions of civil rights could not defend him. This would seem to be the case given that B.J. Clinton's actions were initially directed at defeating a Federal Civil Rights Lawsuit brought against him by Paula Jones (a person and therefore ostensibly entitled to Civil Rights). There was, however, only an eerie silence on the part of the usual lions of Civil Rights.

Cheryl Mills, a youthful black female attorney on the WhiteHouse legal team, spoke to the issue of Civil Rights before the Senate. She stated unequivocally that Civil Rights in America were *not impaired* by the actions of the President in lying and causing others to lie in order to defeat the Federal Civil Rights lawsuit against the President. The collective sigh of relief by Democrat Senators actually blew open the doors of the Senate Chamber. For Cheryl Mills was, indeed, both Black and

Female in addition to being an attorney. She was a clear authority on the matter.

Cheryl Mills went on to remind us that; "Thomas Jefferson, Frederick Douglas, Abraham Lincoln, John F Kennedy, Martin Luther King Jr.: we revere these men, But they were not perfect men. They made human errors . . ." Thankfully Cheryl spared us any rhymes or rap ditties she may have composed on the theme, although doing so might have been just as meaningful as her testimony and would have celebrated diversity, the cornerstone of our Republic.

Barbara Robinson, a columnist and, as a black woman who wears somewhat odd baseball caps, a complete authority on matters of Civil Rights, wrote a clear and convincing defense of Billy Jeff Clinton in the Las Vegas Review Journal. Clearly fighting the Good Fight against the Politics of Personal Destruction, she pointed out that the House Managers prosecuting the President were *all white men*. How could 13 *all white men* represent America? They don't *look* like America. *Do* they?

Barbara correctly pointed out that not only were the white men *white*, but they represented upper-middle class communities like rural Georgia and Arkansas. She further pointed out that they were (and I ask you now to have children leave the room) *competitive* white men. Competitive white men who would have you believe that their actions were based on (again, shield your eyes) *principle*. Barbara properly concluded that these 13 white competitive principled men were *frightening*.

And frightening they are. And thankful we were to Barbara for heralding this threat to justice.

(Unfortunately Barbara was, due to editorial constraints, unable to provide us with her insights as to how these frightening competitive principled white men differed from the competitive principled white men who fought and died by the thousands for Civil Rights in the Civil War. Or how they differed from the competitive principled white men who risked everything, including their lives, in standing up and acting for civil rights during the 60's. We can all look forward to Barbara's future columns in which she will, no doubt, explain those important differences to us.)

Barbara did have time to contrast those 13 frightening competitive principled white men with the WhiteHouse defense team. She pointed out that the WhiteHouse team was inclusive. It included a white man in a wheelchair. Clearly, being in a wheelchair can render even a potentially frightening white man non-frightening. It included a "brilliant attorney" and "sista" personified by Cheryl Mills. Barbara lauded the defense of the TrailerPark President that was elucidated by the brilliant legal minds of Maxine Waters and Sheila Jackson Lee in the House of Representatives. Barbara expanded this list of luminaries by commenting that Rep. Alcee L. Hastings, an African American who had been impeached and removed from the federal bench and subsequently elected to congress, felt the impeachment hearings had "gone far enough". In closing Barbara correctly pointed out that Professor Alan Dershowitz, Felix Frankfurter Professor of Law, stated on "Larry King Live" that he "hated" Bob Barr, one of the white House managers.

The Race Card case is crystal clear. But let's score it, just for fun.

13 Frightening Principled Competitive White Men, versus;

3 Black Women
1 Guy in a Wheelchair
1 Impeached African American Judge, and,
1 Jewish Professor who "hates" one of the 13 white men.

The White Guys didn't stand a chance.

www.jerrymander.com

To order additional copies of **The Wizard of "IS"**, complete the information below:

(or visit www.JerryMander.com for online ordering)

Ship to: (please print)

Name _____

Address_____

City, State, Zip _____

Day phone _____

___copies of *The Wizard of "IS"* @ $14.00 each $ _____

Postage and handling @ $4.00 per book $ _____

Total amount enclosed $ _____

Make checks payable to: *"Jerry Mander Press"*

Send to: **Wizard of IS**
PO Box 5882
Sparks, NV 89432-5882

Credit Card Orders: Visa/MasterCard/Amex/Discover
Call Toll Free: **1-800-356-7798**

* Sales tax is included in the purchase price for books shipped to Nevada addresses.